Single-Session Therapy and Anxiety

Single-Session Therapy and Anxiety

An In-depth Analysis of a Single Session

Windy Dryden, PhD

Onlinevents Publications

First edition published by Onlinevents Publications

Copyright (c) 2025 Windy Dryden and Onlinevents Publications

Windy Dryden
136 Montagu Mansions, London W1U 6LQ

Onlinevents Publications
38 Bates Street, Sheffield, S10 1NQ
www.onlinevents.co.uk
help@onlinevents.co.uk

First edition 2025

ISBN: 978-1-914938-39-9

Contents

*This book is dedicated to the
memory of my mother, Lilian
Denbin and Elizabeth's mother,
Rita Elizabeth Cardigan.*

Preface

In my previous books for Onlinevents, I presented an overview of Single-Session Therapy in the first chapter, continued with a chapter on the problem/issue area to which SST was being applied in the book (e.g. regret or procrastination) and then devoted several chapters where in each chapter I commented on a verbatim transcript of my work with a volunteer seeking single-session help for the designated problem or issue. Then, I discussed the themes that emerged from the presented therapeutic work and from the feedback provided by each volunteer three months after they had their session (see Dryden, 2023, 2024a).

In this book, I thought that I would do something different. Thus, in Chapter 1, I present the verbatim transcript of a single session that I did with Elizabeth,[1] but do so without commentary. I want you, the reader, to consider the work that I did with Elizabeth in this session without having first read an overview of SST and the way I work with anxiety issues.[2] In Chapter 2, I

---

[1] The volunteer chose the name which is not her real name. I did not know until I had finished the book and suggested to Elizabeth that we dedicate it to the memories of our respective mothers – who both featured in the session – that 'Elizabeth' was her mother's middle name. Readers will make of this what they will.

[2] I recently came across a book entitled *Annotated Psychotherapy: A Session by Session Look at How a Therapist Thinks* (Makover, 2024). In that book, the author presents and comments on a number of transcripts of therapy sessions, each showing how an experienced therapist *might* conduct the session. In other words, the dialogues

present SST, how I work with anxiety and the ideas that inform that work in a way that can be linked to the session with Elizabeth, which I present again with detailed linking commentary Thus, you can compare your thoughts about the session having read it in Chapter 1 with your re-reading of it in Chapter 3. In Chapter 4, I present, in full, Elizabeth's follow-up questionnaire, which was completed three months after our session. In Chapter 5, I reflect on some issues that my work with Elizabeth raises, including her reflections where appropriate, and make some concluding remarks.

My decision to feature one session in this book was influenced by the fact that many important features of my work with anxiety can be found in that session. I also wanted you to compare your views of the session before and after reading the material on SST and how I work with anxiety.

On this latter point, as with my other books on SST, I do not advocate that you practise SST with anxiety issues in the manner that I do. Rather, my goal is for you to see how one practitioner approaches the task of helping someone with an issue that is among the most commonly presented to therapists and therapy agencies.

Windy Dryden
London, Eastbourne
April 2025

---

presented were fictitious. By contrast, the transcript of the session that I had with Elizabeth that I present and discuss in this book is real, not made up.

1

The Session with Elizabeth without Commentary

Date: 26/02/24
Time: 39 minutes 2 secs

Windy: Hi Elizabeth, nice to meet you.

Elizabeth: Hello. Nice to meet you too.

Windy: What's your understanding of the purpose of our conversation this evening?

Elizabeth: So, I'm a volunteer to bring to you an anxiety that I have and for you to demonstrate how you'd work with me.

Windy: And what's in it for you?

Elizabeth: I'd like to experience therapy with you and volunteer and also to see if there can be something that can help me with my particular anxiety so that I can take something away and work with it and also help clients as well.

Windy: What would you like to take away from our conversation, Elizabeth?

Elizabeth: More of a deeper understanding of the anxiety and something, some tools I suppose or techniques that I can use to, I don't know, just try to de-escalate it when it's actually happening.

Windy: So, do we need to understand first and then tools and techniques later?

Elizabeth: Yeah. I'd like to understand first, yeah.

Windy: So, let's see if we can both understand. Over to you, then.

Elizabeth: So, you want to know about the anxiety I have?

Windy: Please.

Elizabeth: It's health anxiety. Quite severe. And I've had it for a long time, ever since I can remember, actually, as a child. I've always had it. It has got louder sometimes, quieter sometimes, but it's always there, because obviously I live in my body. And it's everywhere I look it's about health, health, health, health.

Windy: Sorry, everywhere you look? What do you mean?

Elizabeth: It's on the TV, radio, newspapers, which I try to not look at, like adverts. I just feel that everyone's talking about health. It just feels very overwhelming.

Windy: Have you ever been concerned but not anxious about your health?

Elizabeth: Yes. I have had times when I've had concerns. Not often but, yeah, when you said that earlier on, I thought, 'Yeah, actually I do know the difference between.'

Windy: Tell me the difference for you?

Elizabeth: A concern would be it feels more rational, it feels that, OK, I'm on top of this health concern. It might just be like a regular check-up that you have and I don't feel so anxious. I can manage it, but, when I'm really anxious, I feel completely dysregulated, if that's the word to use, and there's just no rational thought. I'm dead, basically. I'm dead when I'm really anxious. I've written my letters to my children that I'm dying and I'm gonna die. And there's a big difference between it.

Windy: Yeah. Let me see if I can understand what you're doing when you're concerned but not anxious, so maybe we can actually draw something from that, since you have had some successful experience of doing that. Can you think of a time when you were concerned but not anxious about your health?

Elizabeth: Yes.... Let me think of something. I'm in good health, actually. So, say for instance, I had to go and have a test for something, like just a female test, and then they said, 'Oh, you've got to come back in six months' time.' So, there was a concern. So, coming back in six months was fine because I hadn't left it; there was no avoidance there. I was able to keep on top of it, not avoid it, 'cos I'm a massive avoider.

Windy: So, you notice then that there's a connection between avoidance and anxiety, and non-avoidance and health?

Elizabeth: Yeah, I did. I felt normal, I felt in control, I felt quite – I don't know if powerful's the word, but I felt on top of it.

Windy: When you felt powerful, are there any images that come to mind that would demonstrate your power?

Elizabeth: I felt like an adult, like a sensible adult.

Windy: Yeah. So that gives you a sense of power.

Elizabeth: Mmm [yes].

Windy: So we may be able to draw on those two principles if we can bring to your issue, your observation that, when you face up to things, that that is useful to you, helpful to you and, when you access the part of you that's an adult, that gives you a sense of power. So those are the two things that you have in your locker, so to speak. Is that right?

Elizabeth: Yeah. It's a very different feeling. It's like that feeling is very different to the other one.

Windy: Sure. So, are you currently anxious about your health at the moment?

Elizabeth: I would say that there's an underlying trickle. I haven't got any symptoms, there's nothing I need apart from going to have a general blood test which I'm avoiding. I've avoided it since September.

Windy: OK. So, would that be a good goal for you?

Elizabeth: Yes.

Windy: To maybe go for your blood test?

Elizabeth: Even the word 'test' makes me feel anxious.

Windy: Can you say the word 'test'?

Elizabeth: Test.

Windy: Sorry.

Elizabeth: Test. Blood test.

Windy: I'm using my 'deaf old man' technique on you.

Elizabeth: Blood test.

Windy: Blood test, right. So how does it feel to say that out loud repetitively, by the way?

Elizabeth: I've got a sense of humour, so laughter always diminishes it a little bit. It's the waiting I can't stand. I'm not worried about the blood test, having it done. I find it very difficult to tolerate waiting. I find that difficult. They're testing for something, aren't they, that's not right.

Windy: OK. I don't know the context of that, but, since we're hopefully gonna encourage you to go into non-avoidant mode, when would you like to take the test?

Elizabeth: End of March.

Windy: That's your goal, then, to take the test?

Elizabeth: Yeah.

Windy: Have you booked it?

Elizabeth: I booked it twice and cancelled.

Windy: OK.

Elizabeth: It's just a general. I asked for the blood test.

Windy: Is this privately or NHS?

Elizabeth: No. I just went to my doctor at the NHS and said, 'I'd like a general MOT.'

Windy: OK. And so, when are you going to request that again?

Elizabeth: … I don't know.

Windy: Tomorrow.

Elizabeth: I'll do it tomorrow.

Windy: Well, what a good suggestion there. Fantastic. Do you have a good relationship with your practice?

Elizabeth: I used to have. Obviously, it all changed with Covid and stuff. I used to have a really lovely doctor there and I wasn't quite as scared of having tests 'cos she had a lovely manner about her. But she left with burnout 'cos everyone wanted to see her.

Windy: What was it about her manner that was helpful to you?

Elizabeth: She was very motherly, and I just didn't feel scared with her. She encouraged me. I just felt safe with her.

Windy: OK. Can I ask you a question? Any question I ask you, you don't have to answer, of course, but let me ask you a question: are you a mother?

Elizabeth: Yes.

Windy: What kind of mother are you?

Elizabeth: Very nurturing, protective worrier.

Windy: How about if we go for the two out of three there and maybe see if you can use those two qualities to replicate what the doctor did for you and maybe mother yourself a little bit?

Elizabeth: Hmm mmm [yes].

Windy: What would that sound like? So, there you are, you've booked your test for the end of March and there you are in the room. What does it sound like to mother yourself?

Elizabeth: 'Everything's gonna be fine. If there is anything wrong, you'll be OK because we can sort it together.' That's what the mothering would say to me, yeah.

Windy: OK. Can I suggest a little modification to that, see how you take that, and add the words 'in all probability'?

Elizabeth: In all probability?

Windy: Yeah. In other words, we can't know for absolute certain.

Elizabeth: Right, OK, yeah.

Windy: How do you feel about adding that little ingredient, in a motherly way?

Elizabeth: … I suppose that makes it feel more realistic and, like you said, we can't have certainty, can we? It feels good, actually, 'in all probability'.

Windy: In all probability. OK, so maybe you can bring that
              to the table: in all probability. Have you ever been
              ill?

Elizabeth: Yeah. I've had operations. I know where it starts. It
              starts with my childhood. I know where it started. I
              have had operations and tests come back that
              could've been a bit iffy but they weren't. I've had
              about four operations, but really nothing sinister,
              thank God.

Windy: Yeah, OK. What was that?

Elizabeth: I just thank God and pray, 'Thank God.'

Windy: Is that a comfort to you?

Elizabeth: Yeah, it is.

Windy: So, one of the things I want to suggest to you: maybe
              comfort's important but comfort in all probability.
              What would you do if they did find something
              sinister? What do you think you'd do?

Elizabeth: Oh God, I'd fall to pieces.

Windy: And then what would you do?

Elizabeth: ... Well, straight away I think of my children. ...
[*Pause*] What would I do?

Windy: Yeah. There you are in pieces.

Elizabeth: I'd panic. I'd have a panic attack.

Windy: Right, and then what?

Elizabeth: ... Well, I suppose I'd come down from the panic
attack and maybe I'd be depressed. I don't know.

Windy: You'd be depressed?

Elizabeth: Or I might ... fight it and do what I can. I don't
know, really.

Windy: OK. What would you do? We're having the scenario
now, might as well. So, initially, you'll go to pieces,
have a panic attack, then you'll be thinking of your
children. By the way, if you didn't have children,
would you still be anxious?

Elizabeth: Not as much, no.

Windy: You wouldn't?

Elizabeth: Not as much. Definitely not.

Windy: OK. How old are your children?

Elizabeth: They're twins and they're coming up to 28.

Windy: So, what about if we bring your children into it, 'cos
                it sounds like that's an important ingredient, isn't it,
                bringing your children into it? Actually, it often is,
                as a matter of fact. So, what is it about your
                children?

Elizabeth: I can't bear the thought of them having to suffer if
                I'm suffering and I can't bear the thought of leaving
                them in this world without me.

Windy: What would happen to them if they didn't have you?

Elizabeth: ... [*Long pause*] Well, they'd be sad.

Windy: And then what?

Elizabeth: ... I suppose they'd come to terms with it.

Windy: How would you feel about that?

Elizabeth: I'd be glad. I'd be really happy if I felt that, yeah.
                Well, not happy, but reassured.

Windy: Reassured.

Elizabeth: Yeah, they'd cope.

Windy: What kind of twins are they? Are they in the house somewhere?

Elizabeth: No, they've left. Well, they come backwards and forwards, but they rent somewhere and then backwards and forwards, yeah. They're not here.

Windy: What kind of women are they?

Elizabeth: Mature. One of them's got health anxiety and gets quite anxious. The other one has got it a little bit but not quite as much; she's much more level-headed. They're independent. They cope. They're clever, intelligent, lots of friends. We talk every day, sometimes three times a day. We text every day.

Windy: OK. So, here's the scenario that I'm going to put to you. We know you're going to die. We're all going to die. But we don't know where, we don't know when. But let's suppose that you tell them and they're very sad and you're very sad, but you have a sense that they have a resilience about them that they could bring to their lives. And they'll miss their mum.

I never knew my grandmother, but my mother had a little cry about losing her mum every day. Then, she got on with her life. They might be like that. They would miss their mum but they've got on with their life. Are they married at all?

Elizabeth: No.

Windy: Do they have any interest in having a family?

Elizabeth: Yeah, they do have an interest in having a relationship and a family of their own.

Windy: OK. So what's the chances of that happening? Shall we have two scenarios here? One is they ain't gonna cope and that's it. They're dead, that's the end of their life. They're spending the rest of their life grieving and not going to work and in bits and pieces. Or they will be bereft without their mum but they'll be sad and they'll be able to move on and be resilient and live life and still remember their mum but actually get on with their life. Now, which version do you have when you're anxious?

Elizabeth: The first one where I think that they're not gonna cope and who are they going to speak to when they're worried.

Windy: Yes. OK, who are they going to speak to when they're worried?

Elizabeth: … Well, friends, each other, close friends of mine.

Windy: What do you do for a living?

Elizabeth: I am actually a counsellor.

Windy: Is it possible that they might choose to speak to a counsellor?

Elizabeth: Oh yes, they would.

Windy: OK, fine. You see, one of the things is, if you allow yourself to have the first response but then use that as a cue to have the second response, like, 'I might die one day and, if I do, my thoughts are they'll be crushed but they'll recover, they'll grieve, they'll get on with their life, they'll be resilient.' And, if you knew that, if you could see that from the grave, how would you feel?

Elizabeth: I'd feel much more reassured that they can lead a really balanced life, happy and all the different things without me.

Windy: So, what would happen if you practised that now?

Elizabeth: How do I do that?

Windy: By doing exactly what I said. Recognise that your first response is, 'They'll be crushed,' and then their second response and you build up a picture. Do you draw at all?

Elizabeth: Yeah, I love writing and drawing.

Windy: Write and draw what happens next.

Elizabeth: Yeah.

Windy: That's how you do it. Develop that, because what happens with you is you have this sense, 'Oh my God, I'm going to die,' and, 'Oh my God, my children,' close the book, avoid, anxiety continues. Keep the book open, Chapter 1 is, 'I'll collapse, they'll collapse,' Chapter 2 is they start to get themselves together, they live a life, there'll be resilience, they'll be sad, and develop that idea, practise that.

Elizabeth: Yeah, that feels good. I could definitely do that, yeah. I could write it, 'cos I love writing.

Windy: That's right. Write it, draw it, sing it. And you can bring your individuality to this, 'cos after all, Elizabeth: 'You're not a number. You're a free man.' Do you know that quote?

Elizabeth: Yeah.

Windy: So, we want to bring your individuality to this. So what have we got? OK, here's the biggie. Let's go back to one of the things you said before: 'I can't stand the wait.' What is it about the wait that you can't stand?

Elizabeth: … That I'm waiting for someone, like the doctor, to ring me and my heart's gonna jump out of my mouth and they're just gonna tell me something really terrible.

Windy: And then what?

Elizabeth: And then I've got to then go to the doctor's. I find it even difficult driving past the doctor's sometimes. I have to turn my head.

Windy: OK. Can we agree that, when you drive past the doctor's, you turn to the doctor's? Well, keep your head on the road, we don't want you to have a crash.

Elizabeth: Yes, I will be in danger.

Windy: Indeed, yeah, but you know what I mean. Because what do we know about avoidance? Increases or decreases anxiety?

Elizabeth: … It increases mine.

Windy: Right. So, what do we need to do?

Elizabeth: Face it and, like you say, when I drive past, look at it. I did start that once. As I walked past I said, 'Thank you for all those doctors in there,' 'cos I did have to spend a lot of time there at one point.

Windy: So, again, if you say, 'If there's bad news,' and it's only an 'if', is the uncertainty part of the waiting that you can't stand?

Elizabeth: Oh yeah, I can't bear it.

Windy: You can't bear uncertainty?

Elizabeth: I'm not scared of death any more. I used to be terribly, but since my mum past, I'm not scared of death. I'm scared of dying younger and leaving my children. But the actual death I'm not scared any more 'cos I actually have worked on myself with that.

Windy: Right, now you can work on yourself with what we've spoken about tonight, can't you? The idea that, obviously you wouldn't want to leave your adult women offspring – do you see the different language that I'm using here: adult women offspring versus children? Why do you think I made that shift?

Elizabeth: Well, because it's true, they are adult women offspring. It's like I see them as children that are needy and vulnerable and can't live without me.

Windy: Exactly. Is that how you want them to be?

Elizabeth: No, because that's how I've been with my mum. I do not want that. I don't want that.

Windy: That's right. So, the first thing to do is to recognise that you need to let go of that idea that they are needy children who can't do without you, and help yourself to see that they are what?

Elizabeth: Mature women, adult who are independent offspring.

Windy: Offspring, right.

Elizabeth: And they'll grieve, and they'll cope.

Windy: That's right. So, let's go back to the idea of what it is. Is it the uncertainty, the waiting period? What is it you think you can't stand?

Elizabeth: … It's like I jump every time the phone pings if I'm waiting for something. … [*Pause*] The not knowing. I can't stand the not knowing. I just wanna know straight away.

Windy: Right, OK. That's understandable. But it's your attitude towards uncertainty that's the issue, not the uncertainty itself.

Elizabeth: Right.

Windy: So, I often say to people, 'You don't have an uncertainty problem. You've got an attitude towards uncertainty problem.' Here are the choices, as far as I can see them. Would you be interested in my take on this?

Elizabeth: Mmm [yes].

Windy: Here are the choices. What do we know? We know that you don't like not knowing when it comes to your health. Fine. Nothing wrong with that. We know that you're anxious. Now, let's have a look at which attitude you have towards uncertainty of the two that I'm gonna put to you. One is this: 'I would like to know that everything's OK, but I don't need to know. Not knowing's uncomfortable but bearable.' Or: 'I would like to know that everything's OK and I need to know and I can't stand not knowing.' Now, which attitude do you think you have?

Elizabeth: The second one.

Windy: And what would happen if you had the first?

Elizabeth: Well, it would be so much more functional, 'cos, even when you were talking about my children, I felt the anxiety leave my stomach. When you said, 'Look at them right now. They're not needy, vulnerable children.' So that made me feel better. I felt more centred. And then, as soon as I go back to the, 'Oh, I can't bear this. I can't stand it,' I can just feel the anxiety just rising up in my chest.

Windy: So, recognise that your first response would be, 'I've got to know and I can't stand it.' That's not the problem. It's how you respond to that. So let's have a look what you can bring to the table. What are some of your strengths as a person?

Elizabeth: … I'm very empathetic, I'd say I cope very well in a crisis, strangely enough.

Windy: What enables you to cope in a crisis?

Elizabeth: … I think I've got resilience. I'm a very practical thinker. I can get things done. I can sort it.

Windy: Are you determined?

Elizabeth: Yes.

Windy: What would happen if you brought your resilience
               and your determination to developing the attitude, 'I
               don't like not knowing. I'd like to know. I don't
               need to know. Not knowing is uncomfortable but
               not terrible. It's not unbearable'? What would
               happen if you brought your resilience and your
               determination to developing those ideas?

Elizabeth: I think I'd be a less anxious person. I think I would
               enjoy life more. I wouldn't have this constant dread
               that I'm waiting for something. Well, it's not
               constant, it's a lot of the time that I'm waiting for
               something bad to happen to me. I think I would live
               in the moment more.

Windy: Yeah, that's right. And, so what I'm gonna suggest
               to you is daily practice of that idea and using every
               opportunity to face what you've been avoiding,
               because we know from your testimony that facing
               things has actually helped you to deal with this
               particular problem in the past. It's when you avoid,
               which is understandable because that's the
               empathetic bit. That's your first response. It doesn't
               have to be your last response, avoidance. What I
               say: avoid the avoidance. You can actually do a U-
               turn. But your first port of call's gonna be that,
               understandably, but it doesn't have to be the next
               port of call. And you can really say, 'Right, OK, let
               me face this. I don't like not knowing, but I can

stand it and, if there is anything wrong, then I'll deal with it. And, if I do die, that would be tragic for me and the kids, but they will survive that.' And, so you can actually start to break the legacy that you were brought up with.

Elizabeth: ... [*Pause*] Yeah, 'cos it's a legacy, definitely.

Windy: Yeah, it sounds like a legacy.

Elizabeth: It is, yeah. And I know that I project a lot of my feelings towards my relationship with my mum towards them. I know I do that.

Windy: Yeah. What were some of your feelings about your mum that you're projecting, do you think?

Elizabeth: That I couldn't live without her, when something happened to her.

Windy: And what did you find out?

Elizabeth: It's been very difficult, like super-duper difficult, like horrendous, but it's five years on and I've got to live on for her. And she left me a letter anyway to make sure I did. So I feel that I completely shocked myself. I feel quite emotional saying this now. But... I've actually shocked myself that I ... do function without her.

Windy: Right. And how well do you function without her?

Elizabeth: I cry every day.

Windy: So did my mum.

Elizabeth: Yeah. I cry every day.... She's a very strong woman.

Windy: So, what can you take from that experience to actually function even better? What are some of the things that you may not be doing that you might consider doing for yourself?

Elizabeth: ... [*Pause*] I suppose to face up to things, not avoid, and also ... [*pause*] it's like I want to change the narrative of what you've just said, of my adult children. I can start changing the narrative. My narrative, my story's mine with my mum and I don't want that legacy to carry on. I really don't.

Windy: No. But you did change your narrative. You've changed it. You're functioning. You shocked yourself. You're functioning.

Elizabeth: Yes, I did.

Windy: And so, maybe you can shock yourself even more by doing things that would indicate, 'Hey, I'm functioning even more.' And that's what I'm saying. Is there anything that you could be doing that would indicate that to you?

Elizabeth: Yes. I think I would start to enjoy my life a bit more.

Windy: What kinds of things would you be doing?

Elizabeth: Going out more. I know what it is, it's doing the things … that I haven't done since she passed.

Windy: Like what?

Elizabeth: Looking at photos.

Windy: Of her?

Elizabeth: Yeah. Just enjoying her when she was well.

Windy: That's right, and also allowing yourself to be sad while you enjoy.

Elizabeth: Yeah.

Windy: It's both/and. It's not either/or.

Elizabeth: Yeah. It's going places that I avoid.

Windy: OK. Let's have a look at where you're avoiding that you would like to go.

Elizabeth: OK. A place?

Windy: Yeah.

Elizabeth: I'm from East London. My family are from East London.

Windy: Whereabouts?

Elizabeth: We're from Stepney.

Windy: OK. You're a Stepney girl?

Elizabeth: Yeah.

Windy: I'm a Hackney boy.

Elizabeth: Oh yeah, I know Hackney really well. So the markets. My family were market traders and I want to go back to those places where my mum went.

Windy: OK. So why don't you go? Do you have a mobile phone? Here's my invitation: send me a picture of you in Stepney.

Elizabeth: Yeah, I will do.

Windy: Send it to me by email. I'd love to see.

Elizabeth: Yeah. I'd love to go back to our house.

Windy: Fine. And what do you think you'd feel by going back to your house?

Elizabeth: I'd just feel more connected to my mum 'cos I'm not burying it. I just wanna bring her back but in that way.

Windy: Yeah, OK. And can you have that connection and still recognise that she's dead?

Elizabeth: I don't use the word 'dead', but you've done it now.

Windy: Well, what do you use?

Elizabeth: Passed away.

Windy: Alright, that's fine.

Elizabeth: I do feel connected to her and I really do, yeah. I talk to her every day.

Windy: OK. Do you ever talk to yourself every day without talking to your mum?

Elizabeth: … She's always there, so I don't know. I think I do. Yeah, I do.

Windy: Moving forward, what kind of relationship do you want to have with your mum that's healthy for you and will aid you in dealing with your health anxiety?

Elizabeth: I want to be a bit more adult to adult with her. I wanna be a bit more independent. She came to all hospital appointments. Obviously, I'm 58, so she died – I said it then – five years ago.

Windy: How does it feel to say it, by the way?

Elizabeth: … [*Long pause*] A bit weird to say it 'cos I don't say it.

Windy: Yeah. It just popped out.

Elizabeth: It just came out, yeah. I very rarely say it. I do sound very childlike when I say it 'cos even before she got ill she would come to the dentist with me, all doctors' appointments, everything.

Windy: And what do you think that said to you about your own resilience?

Elizabeth: I can't cope without her.

Windy: Exactly. Now, do you go to your adult daughters' appointments with them?

Elizabeth: They don't let me, no.

Windy: They don't let you. But you would if you could?

Elizabeth: I would, but there's a part of me that I'm glad they do it 'cos I have brought them up that they do. So I'm glad that they do do that.

Windy: So, I think that one of the things we've talked about, isn't it, this idea that you've developed that you thought at one point you couldn't do without your mum.

Elizabeth: Absolutely.

Windy: You're now learning that you can and that you want to have a more adult-to-adult relationship with her. What was her first name?

Elizabeth: Rita.

Windy: Can you call her Rita?

Elizabeth: Yeah, Rita.

Windy: In your conversations with her?

Elizabeth: Yeah, I could do. Rita.

Windy: Rather than what?

Elizabeth: Mum.

Windy: That's right. One way of having an adult relationship with your mum, to change the language. Call her Rita. What did she used to call you?

Elizabeth: My Angel.

Windy: Well, have her call you Elizabeth in this dialogue. You've got My Angel. And so, I think you have learnt, but, even when you learnt it, you had broken away. Now you can continue to actually have that more fun and have an adult relationship with your mum where you call her by her first name, not Mum and My Angel – Rita and Elizabeth. And then you can continue the legacy of showing your kids, your adult female children that they can get by without you and that you can get by without them.

Elizabeth: Yeah.

Windy: And, if you did that and consistently do that, it will be very interesting to see what happens to your health anxiety, particularly if you also learnt to tolerate uncertainty, tolerate the wait and recognise that the way to deal with these things is as a book: Chapter 1 where you do have these initial reactions, but there's a Chapter 2, Chapter 3, Chapter 4 for you and a Chapter 1, Chapter 2, Chapter 3, Chapter 4 for them.

Elizabeth: Yeah.

Windy: OK. So do you wanna summarise what we've done?

Elizabeth: Yeah. For me to summarise?

Windy: Yeah. I'm too old to summarise.

Elizabeth: So, I started the session, presented to you that I've got dreadful health anxiety, couldn't live without my mum, worried about leaving my children if I'm ill and what are they gonna do and how are they gonna cope. My go-to emotion is to panic and think I'm gonna die or everything's gonna be catastrophic if something happens to me. But to get more into that adult part of me and to recognise my children are adults. To be less avoidant. To know that I can have that Chapter 2, and that's really resonated with me. To call my mum by her first name, to have that adult-to-adult relationship. I like what you said about avoid the avoidance. To be more ... present and to try to accept the feelings I have with uncertainty. And that, basically, we will all cope because I have coped. I have coped without my mum being physically here. And I have coped and know that my children will cope if in the probability of whatever the probability is.

Windy: Of what?

Elizabeth: Of me becoming ill and them having to cope.

Windy: Yeah.

Elizabeth: I know they will cope.

Windy: You will die. We don't know where, we don't know when.

Elizabeth: We don't know when. Like that song that you said: *We don't know where, we don't know when.*

Windy: But, as you say, you're not scared of dying.

Elizabeth: No, not now.

Windy: No, because you brought your resilience and your determination, which are real strengths of yours, and you can take those with you to Stepney. You can take the determination and your resilience anywhere you wanna go.

Elizabeth: Yeah, and also the other part is for me to start to enjoy things. I do enjoy life, I do go out. It's not that I don't. It's just that I avoid places. But to enjoy my mum, the continuing bond I've got with her, if you like, to enjoy her before she was ill, where I haven't done that. To enjoy who she is and go to those places.

Windy: And, even though it might be painful, you can still go and rely on your resilience and your determination, because you will be taking those with you.

Elizabeth: Yeah, my resilience and also I can feel sad and happy as well in the same experience.

Windy: Absolutely, yeah. So we didn't do much in our single session, did we? Thank you so much for having this conversation.

Elizabeth: Thank you so much.

2

What Informed My Work with Elizabeth: Single-Session Therapy, Anxiety and Rational Emotive Behaviour Therapy

In this chapter, I will begin by discussing single-session therapy and how I have adapted it to demonstrate this way of working with interested counsellors and psychotherapists. I will then outline my perspective on anxiety, which is informed, in part, by ideas taken from Rational Emotive Behaviour Therapy, which I will also discuss. I don't always draw upon REBT-informed ideas when I do SST in general, but I often do so when people are seeking help with anxiety issues. In presenting SST and my 'take' on anxiety, and how to address it, I will refer to the session that I did with Elizabeth (see the session without comments in Chapter 1) and will link each major point to that session, which can be found in Chapter 3 where I do comment on my work with Elizabeth.[3]

---

[3] When I do this, I will use the following system. When referring to SST-informed ideas, I will use the symbol and acronym '#SST' followed by a number (e.g. **#SST 1**, **#SST 2**, etc.). When referring to general ideas about anxiety, I will use the symbol and abbreviation '#ANX' followed by a number (e.g. **#ANX 1**, **#ANX 2**, etc. Finally,

Single-Session Therapy

Single-Session Therapy (SST) is an intentional endeavour where the therapist and client contract to help the client achieve what they have come for from the session with the understanding that further help is available to them if they want it after they have had the opportunity to implement what they took from the session and have come to an informed decision about whether or not to seek further help (Dryden, 2024b). This differs from the work I do for Onlinevents where a person volunteers for a single session with me related to the topic of the workshop that I am giving (in Elizabeth's case, anxiety). While the goal of the session still concerns helping the person to take away what they have come for, there is no opportunity for further help from me. However, when a person volunteers for a book project related to an Onlinevents workshop, they do have an opportunity to give feedback on the session and what they made of it three months later.

In this section on SST, I will begin by outlining the single-session mindset, discussing how to begin a session, and explaining how to understand the person's nominated problem and related goal. Then, I will discuss the issues that arise when searching for solutions in SST before concluding with how to end the session well. Throughout, I will reference the points discussed with the work I did with Elizabeth.

---

when referring to REBT-informed ideas, I will use the symbol and acronym '#REBT' followed by a number (e.g. **#REBT 1**, **#REBT 2**, etc.).

The Single-Session Therapy Mindset

Perhaps the most important ingredient in the effective practice of SST is for therapists to hold what is known as the single-session therapy mindset (Dryden, 2024b). Indeed, when therapists hold what might be referred to as a 'traditional therapy mindset' where therapy is seen as work undertaken with a client over time, then they struggle to practice SST. What follows is a brief discussion of the elements of the single-session therapy mindset that I find particularly useful when doing live demonstrations of SST.

It Is Possible to Conduct a Session without Prior Knowledge of the Person

I knew nothing about Elizabeth before she volunteered for the session, and we began talking.

Start Therapy from the First Moment

As can be seen, I started working therapeutically with Elizabeth immediately.

View the Session as a Whole, Complete in Itself

While working with Elizabeth, I kept in mind that this was the only time I would be seeing her and that I wanted to end the session with her taking away something meaningful.

Potentially Anyone Can Be Helped in a Single Session

I did not engage Elizabeth in any pre-session assessment to determine her suitability for SST. I make the assumption that anyone can benefit from SST. This does not mean, of course, that everyone will benefit from a single session. Before calling for volunteers in this context, I generally state that a person should volunteer if they have a current issue with which they are struggling that reflects the theme of the workshop (in this case, anxiety) and for which they would like some help. Before a person volunteers, I suggest that they should be mindful of the fact that the session will take place live in front of an online professional audience and that the usual confidentiality principle applies (i.e. what the volunteer and I discuss will be held in confidence). I also mentioned that afterwards, I would send the volunteer a recording and a typed transcript of the session. Also, I made it clear to Elizabeth that I was planning a book on SST and anxiety and would want to include our transcript in the book.[4]

Focus on the Person, Not the Disorder

While Elizabeth sought help for an anxiety issue, I think the session shows that I was focused on her as a person who had an issue with anxiety. I am not interested in whether or not she has

---

[4] After the session, I invited Elizabeth formally to agree to let me use the transcript of the session in this book and that she would offer her written reflections on the session three months after the session took place. She signed a contract to indicate her agreement with these points.

a diagnosable disorder. I offer bespoke help in SST and do not use a protocol to guide my interventions.

The Client–Therapist Relationship Can Be Established Rapidly

I endeavoured to form a working alliance with Elizabeth by focusing on what she wanted to discuss and by helping her set and work towards meeting her session goal.

Be Transparent

Transparency in SST is shown by me being clear with a person about what SST is and what it isn't, what I can do in the session, and what I can't. I did not have to make these clarifications with Elizabeth.

SST Is Client-Led

Elizabeth led the session by indicating what she wanted to discuss and what she wanted to achieve. I was happy to go along with this. Later, I did ask Elizabeth if she wanted to hear my 'take' on how she might help herself using some ideas from REBT and only gave my views once she had agreed.

Identify and Meet the Volunteer's Preference for Being Helped

Elizabeth said that she wanted to understand her issue more deeply and also take away some tools and techniques that she could use afterwards.

Keep in Mind the Importance of Negotiating an End-of-Session Goal with the Client

I did this with Elizabeth and refined this goal as the session unfolded.

Keep in Mind the Importance of Co-creating a Therapeutic Focus and Maintaining It Once It Has Been Created

Elizabeth and I agreed to focus on her health anxiety; I did not need to help her maintain this focus.

Focus on What the Client Has Done Before Concerning the Problem

A client has usually made several attempts to help themself with their problem before seeking help for it. In my session with Elizabeth, I focused more on examples of when she handled her problem well so that we could tease out these ingredients and develop them.

Focus on the Client's Internal Strengths and External Resources

SST is an example of a strengths-based approach to therapy. In the session, Elizabeth says that her strengths are being empathic and coping well in a crisis. In particular, I help her to develop the latter and see how she can use this resource to help her with her nominated issue of health anxiety.

Be Solution-Focused, if Relevant

Solution-focused work is perhaps the most common type of work in SST (Dryden, 2025), and this certainly was a feature of my session with Elizabeth as we worked to identify the tools and techniques she stated she wanted at the outset.

Small May Be Beautiful

A single session is seen as the start of a process of change rather than the end of it, and this was certainly in my mind as I worked with Elizabeth.

Results Are Mainly Achieved Outside the Session

This was certainly the case with Elizabeth. She needs to implement what she learned about dealing with health anxiety from the session to benefit from it.

Encourage Generalisation, Whenever Possible

Helping a client to generalise their learning to other issues is a useful way to help the client get the most from the session. However, there are times when doing so might detract from what the client will take away from the session. In my view, the latter was the case with Elizabeth.

End the Session Well so that the Client Leaves the Session with Their Morale Restored

Ending the session well includes having the client summarise the session and helping them identify what they will use from it in their life. It also involves ensuring that the client doesn't go away with any unfinished business that might interfere with the benefit they derived from the session. You will see how I ended the session with Elizabeth and the thinking behind this in my commentary in Chapter 3.

Beginning the Session

A typical way that I begin a single session is to ask the person for their understanding of the purpose of the conversation that we are about to have [#SST 1]. This ensures that the person and I are on the same page regarding our expectations from the session. Once it is clear that we have shared expectations regarding the session, I will ask the person concerning their goal for the session [#SST 2]. When a client specifies that they want to understand an issue, then I tend to ask them if they just want such understanding or whether they hope such understanding will lead to them addressing the issue [#SST 3]. When this latter is the case, the person is making a distinction between a session-related goal and a problem-related goal [#SST 4].

At this point, we are ready to create a focus for the session [#SST 5]. The focus should contain the issue that the person wants to discuss and the session goal that relates to this issue. If relevant, the focus includes the person's problem-related goal. When a focus has been created, it is my responsibility as therapist to help the client maintain the focus. I usually do this by bringing the client back to the focus gently.[5] Sometimes, I may need to interrupt the client if they stray away from the focus, and gentle guiding back does not work. The best way I have found to do this in SST is to (a) give the client a rationale for making an interruption, (b) obtain the client's agreement to be interrupted, and (c) have them suggest a way that I can best interrupt them.[6]

Understanding the Problem and/or the Solution

Once a focus has been created, I can help myself and the client to understand the issue and, if relevant at this stage, the way they have solved the problem in the past [# SST 6]. The best way I have found of doing this is to ask for a specific example of the problem or when the client used a solution that seemed to work [#SST 7]. In doing the latter, it is particularly important for me

---

[5] I didn't need to do this with Elizabeth.
[6] I didn't need to interrupt Elizabeth.

to help the client identify specifically what was particularly helpful that they 'brought to the table' [#SST 8]. I will subsequently help them to draw on and utilise what they did that was helpful to them.[7] Often, when I am assessing the client's problem or solution, a specific goal emerges from the discussion. Thus, in Elizabeth's case, going for a blood test that she has been avoiding emerges as such a goal [#SST 10]. In SST, helping a client to apply their own strengths to their nominated issue is useful. It is also useful to identify helpful factors provided by others that are relevant to the solution of the problem and to encourage the client to apply these factors to themself. Thus, in assessing Elizabeth's experience of having a blood test, I discovered that she found the 'mothering' approach of her previous doctor to be helpful. I then encouraged her to use this quality with herself [# SST 11].

Searching for Solutions

In looking for solutions, it is important for me as therapist to recognise that my major task here is to introduce novelty into the discussion so that the client stops repeating patterns of thinking and behaviour that will maintain their anxiety issue. One potential solution that I have found useful to discuss with clients involves them seeing their problems from a broader perspective. Particularly in anxiety, people tend to withdraw from or avoid perceived threatening situations, thus depriving themselves of

---

[7] I find using humour helpful throughout SST and show it here to make discussing a difficult topic a bit easier for Elizabeth [# SST 9].

utilising their naturally occurring healthy responses in the context of unfolding time or, in Elizabeth's case, seeing her daughters' naturally occurring healthy responses in a similar timeframe [**#SST 12**]. Once I have helped the client to 'avoid avoidance' they can see that a good outcome is probable towards the end of the process of unfolding time. It is then useful to compare both scenarios side by side. Here, I contrast the 'avoidant-based' scenario, where when a negative event occurs, the person stops thinking about it, with the 'facing' scenario, where when the same negative event occurs, the person thinks about what happens as time unfolds and what they can do within that timeframe to help themself). I then ask the client which scenario they would like to go forward with [**#SST 13**].

In discussing solutions to issues with clients, I have found it useful to encourage them to see that while they may not be able to stop an unhealthy response from starting, they can respond to that initial response in a healthier way, and I do this with Elizabeth [**#SST 14**], and I encourage her to use her preferred modalities of drawing and writing in doing this [**#SST 15**]. A little later, I use my 'book analogy' where this process can be seen as chapters in a book [**#SST 16a**; **#SST 16b**]. Clients often close the book at Chapter 1 and thus maintain their anxiety issue.

Also, in helping clients to construct a solution, I encourage them to redefine relationships to promote growth. This is demonstrated here when I encourage Elizabeth to see her daughters as 'adult offspring' rather than 'children' [**#SST 17a**]. I also suggest that Elizabeth begins to refer to her mother by her first name rather than 'mum' and think of her mother calling her by her first name rather than 'my angel' to facilitate an adult–

adult relationship that will, in turn, facilitate a solution [**#SST 17b**].

I mentioned at the beginning of this chapter that I often draw upon ideas from REBT in helping clients with anxiety in SST. I do so here with Elizabeth, but before I do so, I ask her if she is interested in my 'take' on here issue and what can be done about it [**#SST 18**].

In using REBT-informed ideas, I also encourage the client to draw on their strengths to help them get the most from these ideas [**#SST 19**]. While exploring the issue of strengths, Elizabeth provides more important information about her relationship with her mother and how she may be projecting her own helplessness and neediness in that relationship into her adult daughters. Although we are in the second half of the session, it is important to incorporate this information into the solution [**#SST 20**]. As we explore this, the focus returned to her own ability to cope without her mum. Although Elizabeth has found this very difficult, she has discovered a level of functionality that has shocked her. I then proceed to help her build on this [**#SST 21**]. This is a typical strategy in SST that comes from solution-focused brief therapy (see Ratner, George and Iveson, 2012) and shows the eclectic/integrative nature of this form of therapy delivery.

Another way of promoting the choice of a solution in SST is to encourage the client to change a narrative. If a client's problem has a narrative, their preferred outcome has a different narrative and encouraging the client to make a choice between these narratives can be useful [**#SST 22**].

Usually, it is important to have the client rehearse the solution. I do not do this with Elizabeth, and thinking about it now, while I wish that I had, I think the reason that I didn't was that the solution involved a change in perspective and attitude rather than behaviour, although facing her adversities rather than avoiding them is behavioural in nature (e.g. going back to her birthplace).

Ending the Session

Once a client has developed an action plan to implement their chosen solution, this shows that the end of the session is approaching. When this occurs, I usually ask the client to summarise the session. Although I did not do the above explicitly with Elizabeth, I did so implicitly and thus, I invited her to summarise the session at a similar point [#SST 23]. Once the client has provided a summary, then I will also ask them what they will take away from the session as their summary and takeaways are sometimes different. I did not ask Elizabeth for her takeaways as her summary was already comprehensive. However, I wish I had done so [#SST 24]. Finally, in order to end the session well and to ensure that the client has had an opportunity to tell me something that they might regret later not telling me or to ask me something they might regret later not asking me, I usually give them this opportunity before finishing. I did not do this as I felt that we had reached a good ending. However, again, I wish I had done so [#SST 25].

My Perspective on Understanding Anxiety and on Helping People to Address It

Anxiety is the issue for which clients most frequently seek therapeutic help. This is the case for therapy, in general, and for SST, in particular (Dryden, 2025). Indeed, the word 'anxiety' features in the name of the National Health Service's provision for the treatment of psychological problems in the United Kingdom – 'The NHS Talking Therapies Service for Anxiety and Depression'.

In this section of the chapter, I will discuss what I have to offer clients seeking help with anxiety in SST. This help is often informed by ideas stemming from Rational Emotive Behaviour Therapy (REBT). I will only offer a client my perspective when they are clearly struggling to understand or deal with their anxiety issue. Before I do so, I will ask my client if they are interested in my 'take' on their anxiety issue and how they can deal with it. If they are interested, I will share it. If they are not, I won't. Almost always, however, they are interested in my 'take'.

While, as mentioned above, anxiety is probably the most common emotional problem for which clients seek SST, many of these clients know little about this emotional problem that will help them address it effectively. In outlining the ideas and concepts that I bring to the table when helping clients deal with their anxiety issues, I will refer specifically to my work with Elizabeth.

Non-Anxious Concern Is the Healthy Alternative to Anxiety

REBT makes a distinction between healthy and unhealthy negative emotions. The healthy alternative to anxiety is not the absence of anxiety or a less intense form of anxiety. It is what I call non-anxious concern [#REBT 1]. Anxiety and concern have different behavioural and cognitive concomitants. Thus, anxiety is related to avoidance [#ANX 1] and concern to non-avoidance [#ANX 2]

The Two Main Components of Anxiety and Concern

Anxiety[8] has two major components. First, it is based on a set of attitudes that the person holds towards something that they deem to be threatening [#REBT 2]. According to REBT, these attitudes are deemed to be rigid and extreme in nature [#REBT 3a] – Appendices 1 and 2. Second, it is based on the person's appraisal that they won't be able to deal with the threat. It follows that I may need to help a client with the first, second or both components. Concern is also based on a set of attitudes towards the same adversity. First, according to REBT, these attitudes are deemed to be based on a set of flexible/non-extreme attitudes that the person holds towards the same threat as in anxiety [#REBT 3b] – Appendices 1 and 2. Second, it is based on the person's appraisal that they will be able to deal with the threat.

---

[8] In this section, I will be discussing anxiety, which is psychological in nature. Sometimes, anxiety is related more to medical issues.

The Behavioural and Thinking Concomitants of Anxiety and Non-Anxious Concern

In Appendix 3, the main features of anxiety and non-anxious concern are presented. From this Appendix, it can be seen that both anxiety and non-anxious concern are about threat. In anxiety, as mentioned above, the person processes this threat with rigid/extreme attitudes, while in non-anxious concern, they process the threat with flexible/non-extreme attitudes. It can also be seen from this table that the behavioural and thinking concomitants of anxiety and non-anxious concern are very different, and it is these concomitants that help me as therapist and my client see clearly if the latter is experiencing anxiety or non-anxious concern. If the former, the behavioural and concomitants of non-anxious concern help the client see what they need to do and think as they implement a co-created attitude-based solution to their anxiety problem.

Disturbed Emotional Responses to Anxiety

Quite often, people make themselves disturbed about their anxiety (e.g., ashamed, depressed, guilty, etc.)[9] If this is the case,[10] I, as a therapist, and my client, need to discuss whether they should focus in the session on the client's original anxiety or their meta-emotional disturbance (i.e. their disturbed responses to anxiety) as we may not have time to address both in

---

[9] When a person disturbs themself about their original disturbance, this is known as meta-emotional disturbance.

[10] This did not occur with Elizabeth.

the single session. However, if we do have time, I strive to cover both issues with the client as long as they feel able to take away something meaningful with respect to both problems.

Perhaps the most common form of meta-disturbance with respect to anxiety is anxiety about anxiety. When this happens, and the client wants to focus on this 'secondary' disturbance, I help them identify what it is about their 'primary' anxiety that they consider to be most threatening. I then strive to help the client to appraise this threat more realistically and to see that they can deal with the threat.

In general, when helping a client deal with their meta-disturbance about anxiety, I endeavour to help them in three ways. First, I encourage them to understand that the feeling of anxiety is painful but usually not dangerous. Second, I help them see that they can bear feeling anxious even though they think that they cannot bear it. Third, I invite the person to view anxiety as a sign that they are a fallible human being who is holding a rigid and extreme attitude towards threat. It is not evidence that they are a weak person.

Common Attempts to Deal with Anxiety Often Serve to Maintain It

Since anxiety is a painful emotion which affects several parts of the person's body and physiological functioning, it is natural (but not constructive) for the person to try to get away from these feelings as quickly as possible [#ANX 1] rather than stay in the situation and deal constructively with the threat [#ANX 2].

However, attempts to eliminate anxiety only serve to maintain or increase it. Realistic, mindful acceptance of anxiety is the healthy alternative to elimination. This involves me helping the client acknowledge that they feel anxiety and that it is unpleasant. I then encourage them to let the anxious feelings remain so that they can deal with them constructively and face the threat about which they are anxious.

Similarly, when a client attempts to avoid or withdraw from threat, they, again unwittingly, only serve to maintain their anxiety. Instead, as noted above, they need to face the threat and deal with it effectively [#**ANX 1, ANX2**].

Another way in which the person maintains their anxiety problem is to stay in the closet with respect to the threat that they find anxiety-provoking. Trying to hide from others and from oneself that one is anxious only serves to make one's anxiety problem worse in the long run, and when this happens, I encourage my client to look at the factors that lead them to stay in the closet and the factors they would need to be present for them to come out of the closet. I then work with them to achieve the latter.

Helping the Client to Deal Healthily with the Issue of Loss of Control

One of the most common threats people experience when anxious is loss of control. I have found it useful to help clients who experience such anxiety to consider the following:

- It is important that the client is clear about what they are in control of (largely themself) and what you are not in control of (largely others and events involving others).
- If the client holds a rigid and extreme attitude towards loss of self-control this will lead them to think that they will lose complete control of themself if they begin to lose such control (see Appendix 3).
- If the client holds a flexible and non-extreme attitude towards loss of self-control this will lead them to focus on how to respond when they begin to lose such control. They will tend not to think they will lose complete control of themselves (see Appendix 3).

Helping the Client to Deal Healthily with Uncertainty

Another common threat that people experience when they are anxious is uncertainty [**#ANX 3**]. This was the case with Elizabeth. I have found it useful to help clients who experience such anxiety to consider the following:

- Uncertainty in the face of threat does not on its own lead to anxiety [**#REBT 2**].
- If the client holds a rigid and extreme attitude towards such uncertainty this will lead to anxiety. This attitude will lead them to think that if they do not know they are safe, then they are in danger [**#REBT 3a**].
- If the client holds a flexible and non-extreme attitude towards such uncertainty this will lead to non-anxious concern. This

attitude will lead them to think that they are probably safe even if they do not know for certain that they are [**#REBT 3b**].

- Thus, it is quite probable that the client is safe even when they are facing uncertainty. Uncertainty is not a sign of danger. It is a sign that they are in a state of not knowing. This may be an unpleasant state, but that is all that it is.
- The client should only seek reassurance if they are able to be reassured in the longer term (i.e., they are re-assurable). Continually seeking reassurance when they are not re-assurable, will maintain their anxiety problem [**#REBT 4**].

3

The Session with Elizabeth with Commentary

Date: 26/02/24
Time: 39 minutes 2 secs

Windy: Hi Elizabeth, nice to meet you.

Elizabeth: Hello. Nice to meet you too.

Windy: What's your understanding of the purpose of our conversation this evening? [**#SST 1**]

[*This is my standard opening question when I do an SST demonstration. I am checking that the person's expectations are aligned with mine.*]

Elizabeth: So, I'm a volunteer to bring to you an anxiety that I have and for you to demonstrate how you'd work with me.

[*Elizabeth's response omits what she wants to gain from the session personally. So, I ask her specifically about this.*]

62

Windy: And what's in it for you?

Elizabeth: I'd like to experience therapy with you and volunteer and also to see if there can be something that can help me with my particular anxiety so that I can take something away and work with it and also help clients as well.

[Note that Elizabeth's reasons for volunteering are twofold: to get some help and experience therapy with me. This dual purpose is not unusual in my book projects for Onlinevents as virtually all volunteers are therapists or work in the helping professions.]

Windy: What would you like to take away from our conversation, Elizabeth? [**#SST 2**]

[I am asking Elizabeth for her goal for the session.]

Elizabeth: More of a deeper understanding of the anxiety and something, some tools I suppose or techniques that I can use to, I don't know, just try to de-escalate it when it's actually happening.

Windy: So, do we need to understand first and then tools and techniques later?

[When clients mention that they want to understand their issue better <u>and</u> want some tools and techniques to address the issue, I usually like to sequence these goals with understanding preceding the search for tools/techniques. Understanding and the identification of tools and techniques represent the session goal [#SST 3]. Implementing the tools and techniques so that she can de-escalate in the session represents Elizabeth's problem-related goal [#SST 4].]

Elizabeth: Yeah. I'd like to understand first, yeah.

Windy: So, let's see if we can both understand. Over to you, then.

Elizabeth: So, you want to know about the anxiety I have?

Windy: Please.

Elizabeth: It's health anxiety. Quite severe. And I've had it for a long time, ever since I can remember, actually, as a child. I've always had it. It has got louder sometimes, quieter sometimes, but it's always there, because obviously I live in my body. And it's everywhere I look it's about health, health, health, health.

[Health anxiety is the focus of the session [#SST 5].]

Windy: Sorry, everywhere you look? What do you mean?

Elizabeth: It's on the TV, radio, newspapers, which I try to not look at, like adverts. I just feel that everyone's talking about health. It just feels very overwhelming.

Windy: Have you ever been concerned but not anxious about your health? [**#REBT 1**]

        [In asking this, I am making a distinction between un-anxious concern and anxiety which from my perspective is an important one to make and which is informed by REBT

Elizabeth: Yes. I have had times when I've had concerns. Not often but, yeah, when you said that earlier on, I thought, 'Yeah, actually I do know the difference between.'

Windy: Tell me the difference for you?

        [Here, I invite Elizabeth to give her own distinction between anxiety and concern rather than give the REBT-informed distinction. I would have provided the latter if I needed to.]

Elizabeth: A concern would be it feels more rational, it feels that, OK, I'm on top of this health concern. It might just be like a regular check-up that you to have and I don't feel so anxious. I can manage it, but, when I'm really anxious, I feel completely dysregulated, if that's the word to use, and there's just no rational thought. I'm dead, basically. I'm dead when I'm really anxious. I've written my letters to my children that I'm dying and I'm gonna die. And there's a big difference between it.

Windy: Yeah. Let me see if I can understand what you're doing when you're concerned but not anxious, so maybe we can actually draw something from that, since you have had some successful experience of doing that. Can you think of a time when you were concerned but not anxious about your health? [#SST 6, #SST 7]

[*Here, I am inviting Elizabeth to describe a situation where she was handling a health issue with un-anxious concern. As I say in my response to her, the purpose of doing so is to help her to use what she has already done that has been helpful to her.*]

Elizabeth: Yes.... Let me think of something. I'm in good health, actually. So, say for instance, I had to go and have a test for something, like just a female test, and then they said, 'Oh, you've got to come back in six months' time.' So, there was a concern. So, coming back in six months was fine because I hadn't left it;

there was no avoidance there. I was able to keep on top of it, not avoid it, 'cos I'm a massive avoider.

Windy: So, you notice then that there's a connection between avoidance and anxiety [**#ANX 1**], and non-avoidance and healthy concern? [**#ANX 2**]

[*I am using Elizabeth's example to develop the differences between the two emotional states.*]

Elizabeth: Yeah, I did. I felt normal, I felt in control, I felt quite – I don't know if powerful's the word, but I felt on top of it.

Windy: When you felt powerful, are there any images that come to mind that would demonstrate your power?

[*Asking for images that the person associates with a positive state is often therapeutic.*]

Elizabeth: I felt like an adult, like a sensible adult.

Windy: Yeah. So that gives you a sense of power.

Elizabeth: Mmm [yes].

Windy: So, we may be able to draw on those two principles if we can bring to your issue, your observation that, when you face up to things, that that is useful to you, helpful to you and, when you access the part of you that's an adult, that gives you a sense of power. So those are the two things that you have in your locker, so to speak. Is that right? [#SST 8]

[*Here, I bring together two factors that Elizabeth has used in the past that can be helpful to her as she addresses her health anxiety.*]

Elizabeth: Yeah. It's a very different feeling. It's like that feeling is very different to the other one.

Windy: Sure. So, are you currently anxious about your health at the moment?

Elizabeth: I would say that there's an underlying trickle. I haven't got any symptoms, there's nothing I need apart from going to have a general blood test which I'm avoiding, I've avoided since September.

Windy: OK. So, would that be a good goal for you?

Elizabeth: Yes.

Windy: To maybe go for your blood test?

[*I am suggesting a particular specific goal first mentioned by Elizabeth.*]

Elizabeth: Even the word 'test' makes me feel anxious.

Windy: Can you say the word 'test'?

Elizabeth: Test.

Windy: Sorry.

Elizabeth: Test. Blood test.

Windy: I'm using my 'deaf old man' technique on you.

Elizabeth: Blood test.

Windy: Blood test, right. So how does it feel to say that out loud repetitively, by the way?

   [*Here I am using repetition and humour to counter any avoidance that Elizabeth might experience [#SST 9].*]

Elizabeth: I've got a sense of humour, so laughter always diminishes it a little bit. It's the waiting I can't stand. I'm not worried about the blood test, having it done. I find it very difficult to tolerate waiting. I find that difficult. They're testing for something, aren't they, that's not right.

[The 'deaf old man' technique where I pretend not to hear something the client says that is useful clarifies for Elizabeth what she finds particularly anxiety-provoking – waiting to have the blood test.]

Windy: OK. I don't know the context of that, but, since we're hopefully gonna encourage you to go into non-avoidant mode, when would you like to take the test?

Elizabeth: End of March.

Windy: That's your goal, then, to take the test? [**#SST 10**]

Elizabeth: Yeah.

Windy: Have you booked it?

Elizabeth: I booked it twice and cancelled.

Windy: OK.

Elizabeth: It's just a general. I asked for the blood test.

Windy: Is this privately or NHS?

Elizabeth: No. I just went to my doctor at the NHS and said, 'I'd like a general MOT.'

Windy: OK. And so, when are you going to request that again?

Elizabeth: … I don't know.

Windy: Tomorrow.

[*My suggestion is in line with non-avoidance.*]

Elizabeth: I'll do it tomorrow.

Windy: Well, what a good suggestion there. Fantastic. Do you have a good relationship with your practice?

[*I respond humorously as if it were her idea.*]

Elizabeth: I used to have. Obviously, it all changed with Covid and stuff. I used to have a really lovely doctor there and I wasn't quite as scared of having tests 'cos she had a lovely manner about her. But she left with burnout 'cos everyone wanted to see her.

Windy: What was it about her manner that was helpful to you?

Elizabeth: She was very motherly and I just didn't feel scared with her. She encouraged me. I just felt safe with her.

Windy: OK. Can I ask you a question? Any question I ask you, you don't have to answer, of course, but let me ask you a question: are you a mother?

Elizabeth: Yes.

Windy: What kind of mother are you?

Elizabeth: Very nurturing, protective worrier.

Windy: How about if we go for the two out of three there and maybe see if you can use those two qualities to replicate what the doctor did for you and maybe mother yourself a little bit? [# **SST 11**].

[*Here, I take the helpful qualities shown by Elizabeth's doctor (being motherly) and see if she can use her healthy mothering skills with herself.*]

Elizabeth: Hmm mmm [yes].

Windy: What would that sound like? So, there you are, you've booked your test for the end of March and there you are in the room. What does it sound like to mother yourself?

[*I take Elizabeth's agreement and invite her to express out loud what mothering herself would sound like in a specific context - taking the test in March.*]

Elizabeth: 'Everything's gonna be fine. If there is anything wrong, you'll be OK because we can sort it together.' That's what the mothering would say to me, yeah.

Windy: OK. Can I suggest a little modification to that, see how you take that, and add the words 'in all probability'?

Elizabeth: In all probability?

Windy: Yeah. In other words, we can't know for absolute certain.

*[Here, I am guarding against Elizabeth's use of self-reassurance and suggest introducing the concept of probability. I do this because I know that self-reassurance will maintain the Elizabeth's problem not provide a solution to it [#**REBT 4**].]*

Elizabeth: Right, OK, yeah.

Windy: How do you feel about adding that little ingredient, in a motherly way?

Elizabeth: … I suppose that makes it feel more realistic and, like you said, we can't have certainty, can we? It feels good, actually, 'in all probability'.

Windy: In all probability. OK, so maybe you can bring that to the table: in all probability. Have you ever been ill?

Elizabeth: Yeah. I've had operations. I know where it starts. It starts with my childhood. I know where it started. I have had operations and tests come back that could've been a bit iffy but they weren't. I've had about four operations, but really nothing sinister, thank God.

Windy: Yeah, OK. What was that?

Elizabeth: I just thank God and pray, 'Thank God.'

Windy: Is that a comfort to you?

Elizabeth: Yeah, it is.

Windy: So, one of the things I want to suggest to you: maybe comfort's important but comfort in all probability. What would you do if they did find something sinister? What do you think you'd do?

[It is important to view an ingredient like 'comfort' as a double-edged sword. Thus, comfort can be used as self-reassurance, which will perpetuate Elizabeth's problem, or it can be allied to probability, where it can have therapeutic value.]

Elizabeth: Oh God, I'd fall to pieces.

Windy: And then what would you do?

Elizabeth: … Well, straight away I think of my children.… [*Pause*] What would I do?

Windy: Yeah. There you are in pieces.

Elizabeth: I'd panic. I'd have a panic attack.

Windy: Right, and then what?

Elizabeth: … Well, I suppose I'd come down from the panic attack and maybe I'd be depressed. I don't know.

Windy: You'd be depressed?

Elizabeth: Or I might … fight it and do what I can. I don't know, really.

Windy: OK. What would you do? We're having the scenario now, might as well. So, initially, you'll go to pieces, have a panic attack, then you'll be thinking of your children. By the way, if you didn't have children, would you still be anxious?

Elizabeth: Not as much, no.

Windy: You wouldn't?

Elizabeth: Not as much. Definitely not.

Windy: OK. How old are your children?

Elizabeth: They're twins and they're coming up to 28.

[*What I am doing here is to help Elizabeth see that her response to finding something sinister can be seen as a process even if she does not intervene with herself. In doing so, she reveals that her twin daughters are an important ingredient that we have to factor in.*]

Windy: So, what about if we bring your children into it, 'cos it sounds like that's an important ingredient, isn't it, bringing your children into it? Actually, it often is, as a matter of fact. So, what is it about your children?

Elizabeth: I can't bear the thought of them having to suffer if I'm suffering and I can't bear the thought of leaving them in this world without me.

Windy: What would happen to them if they didn't have you?

Elizabeth: … [*Long pause*] Well, they'd be sad.

Windy: And then what? [**#SST 12**]

Elizabeth: … I suppose they'd come to terms with it.

Windy: How would you feel about that?

Elizabeth: I'd be glad. I'd be really happy if I felt that, yeah. Well, not happy, but reassured.

Windy: Reassured.

Elizabeth: Yeah, they'd cope.

Windy: What kind of twins are they? Are they in the house somewhere?

Elizabeth: No, they've left. Well, they come backwards and forwards, but they rent somewhere and then backwards and forwards, yeah. They're not here.

Windy: What kind of women are they?

Elizabeth: Mature. One of them's got health anxiety and gets quite anxious. The other one has got it a little bit but not quite as much; she's much more level-headed. They're independent. They cope. They're clever, intelligent, lots of friends. We talk every day, sometimes three times a day. We text every day.

Windy: OK. So, here's the scenario that I'm going to put to you. We know you're going to die. We're all going to die. But we don't know where, we don't know when. But let's suppose that you tell them and they're very sad and you're very sad, but you have a sense that they have a resilience about them that they could bring to their lives. And they'll miss their mum.

I never knew my grandmother, but my mum had a little cry every day over losing her mum, but then she got on with her life. They might be like that. They would miss their mum, but they'll get on with their life. Are they married at all?

Elizabeth: No.

Windy: Do they have any interest in having a family?

Elizabeth: Yeah, they do have an interest in having a relationship and a family of their own.

Windy: OK. So, what's the chances of that happening? Shall we have two scenarios here? One is they ain't gonna cope and that's it. They're dead, that's the end of their life. They're spending the rest of their life grieving and not going to work and in bits and pieces. Or they will be bereft without their mum but they'll be sad and they'll be able to move on and be resilient and live life and still remember their mum but actually get on with their life. Now, which version do you have when you're anxious? [#SST 13]

[In outlining these two scenarios, I am not only assessing which one Elizabeth has when she is anxious, I am also suggesting that there is a healthier alternative for her.]

Elizabeth: The first one where I think that they're not gonna cope and who are they going to speak to when they're worried.

Windy: Yes. OK, who are they going to speak to when they're worried?

Elizabeth: … Well, friends, each other, close friends of mine.

Windy: What do you do for a living?

Elizabeth: I am actually a counsellor.

Windy: Is it possible that they might choose to speak to a counsellor?

Elizabeth: Oh yes, they would.

Windy: OK, fine. You see, one of the things is, if you allow yourself to have the first response but then use that as a cue to have the second response, like, 'I might die one day and, if I do, my thoughts are they'll be crushed but they'll recover, they'll grieve, they'll get on with their life, they'll be resilient.' And, if you knew that, if you could see that from the grave, how would you feel? [**#SST 14**]

                 [*What I am suggesting to Elizabeth here is that while it is likely that her anxiety response might be her first response she can use that as a cue to move into the second response.*]

Elizabeth: I'd feel much more reassured that they can lead a really balanced life, happy and all the different things without me.

Windy: So, what would happen if you practised that now?

Elizabeth: How do I do that?

Windy: By doing exactly what I said. Recognise that your first response is, 'They'll be crushed,' and then their second response, and you build up a picture. Do you draw at all?

Elizabeth: Yeah, I love writing and drawing.

Windy: Write and draw what happens next [**#SST 15**].

Elizabeth: Yeah.

Windy: That's how you do it. Develop that, because what happens with you is you have this sense, 'Oh my God, I'm going to die,' and 'Oh my God, my children,' close the book, avoid, anxiety continues. Keep the book open, Chapter 1 is, 'I'll collapse, they'll collapse,' Chapter 2 is they start to get themselves together, they live a life, there'll be resilience, they'll be sad, and develop that idea, practise that [**#SST 16**].

[*I use this 'chapters in a book' technique when I want to show that the client's response can be placed in a process-based view where they can let go of factors like avoidance that while bringing immediate relief will only maintain the problem in the longer run.*]

Elizabeth: Yeah, that feels good. I could definitely do that, yeah. I could write it, 'cos I love writing.

Windy: That's right. Write it, draw it, sing it. And you can bring your individuality to this, 'cos after all, Elizabeth: 'You're not a number. You're a free man.' Do you know that quote?

Elizabeth: Yeah.

Windy: So, we want to bring your individuality to this. So what have we got? OK, here's the biggie. Let's go back to one of the things you said before: 'I can't stand the wait.' What is it about the wait that you can't stand?

               [*I have kept in mind that I need to help Elizabeth deal with her adversity of waiting in the context of health tests and I return to this now.*]

Elizabeth: … That I'm waiting for someone, like the doctor, to ring me and my heart's gonna jump out of my mouth and they're just gonna tell me something really terrible.

Windy: And then what?

Elizabeth: And then I've got to then go to the doctor's. I find it even difficult driving past the doctor's sometimes. I have to turn my head.

Windy: OK. Can we agree that, when you drive past the doctor's, you turn to the doctor's? Well, keep your head on the road, we don't want you to have a crash.

Elizabeth: Yes, I will be in danger.

Windy: Indeed, yeah, but you know what I mean. Because what do we know about avoidance? Increases or decreases anxiety?

Elizabeth: … It increases mine.

Windy: Right. So, what do we need to do?

Elizabeth: Face it and, like you say, when I drive past, look at it. I did start that once, as I walked past I said, 'Thank you for all those doctors in there,' 'cos I did have to spend a lot of time there at one point.

[In passing, Elizabeth mentions avoiding looking at the doctors' surgery while driving past. I deal with this by encouraging her to face rather than avoid doing so.]

Windy: So, again, if you say, 'If there's bad news,' and it's only an 'if', is the uncertainty [**#ANX 3**] part of the waiting that you can't stand?

Elizabeth: Oh yeah, I can't bear it.

Windy: You can't bear uncertainty?

Elizabeth: I'm not scared of death any more. I used to be terribly, but since my mum passed, I'm not scared of death. I'm scared of dying younger and leaving my children. But the actual death I'm not scared any more 'cos I actually have worked on myself with that.

Windy: Right, now you can work on yourself with what we've spoken about tonight, can't you? The idea that, obviously you wouldn't want to leave your adult women offspring – do you see the different language that I'm using here: adult women offspring versus children? Why do you think I made that shift? [#SST 17a]

                [*Here, I portray her daughters as adult women offspring rather than children, a term that she uses. I then ask her why I did that.*]

Elizabeth: Well, because it's true, they are adult women offspring. It's like I see them as children that are needy and vulnerable and can't live without me.

Windy: Exactly. Is that how you want them to be?

Elizabeth: No, because that's how I've been with my mum. I do not want that. I don't want that.

Windy: That's right. So, the first thing to do is to recognise that you need to let go of that idea that they are needy children who can't do without you, and help yourself to see that they are what?

Elizabeth: Mature women, adult who are independent offspring.

Windy: Offspring, right.

Elizabeth: And they'll grieve and they'll cope.

Windy: That's right. So, let's go back to the idea of what it is. Is it the uncertainty, the waiting period? What is it you think you can't stand?

Elizabeth: … It's like I jump every time the phone pings if I'm waiting for something. … [*Pause*] The not knowing. I can't stand the not knowing. I just wanna know straight away.

Windy: Right, OK. That's understandable. But it's your attitude towards uncertainty that's the issue, not the uncertainty itself. [**#REBT 2**]

[*It would have been better if I had asked a question such as, 'Do you think it is the uncertainty that produces that reaction or your attitude towards uncertainty?'*]

Elizabeth: Right.

Windy: So, I often say to people, 'You don't have an uncertainty problem. You've got an attitude towards uncertainty problem.' Here are the choices, as far as I can see them. Would you be interested in my take on this? [**#SST 18**]

                 [*Asking the client for permission to give one's 'take' on their issue is important in SST. I could have done this a little earlier. My 'take' is based on REBT, an approach to therapy that informs some of my work. Other therapists will have other 'takes'.*]

Elizabeth: Mmm [yes].

Windy: Here are the choices. What do we know? We know that you don't like not knowing when it comes to your health. Fine. Nothing wrong with that. We know that you're anxious. Now, let's have a look at which attitude you have towards uncertainty of the two that I'm gonna put to you. One is this: 'I would like to know that everything's OK, but I don't need to know. Not knowing's uncomfortable but bearable.' Or: 'I would like to know that everything's OK and I need to know and I can't stand not knowing.' Now, which attitude do you think you have? [**#REBT 3a**; **#REBT 3b**]

Elizabeth: The second one.

Windy: And what would happen if you had the first?

Elizabeth: Well, it would be so much more functional, 'cos, even when you were talking about my children, I felt the anxiety leave my stomach. When you said, 'Look at them right down. They're not needy, vulnerable children.' So, that made me feel better. I felt more centred. And then, as soon as I go back to the, 'Oh, I can't bear this. I can't stand it,' I can just feel the anxiety just rising up in my chest.

Windy: So, recognise that your first response would be, 'I've got to know and I can't stand it.' That's not the problem. It's how you respond to that. So, let's have a look what you can bring to the table. What are some of your strengths as a person? [**#SST 19**].

[*Here, I highlight two points. First, Elizabeth's problem is not her first response but how she responds to that first response. Second, she can bring her strengths 'to the table' in dealing with this first response.*]

Elizabeth: … I'm very empathetic, I'd say I cope very well in a crisis, strangely enough.

Windy: What enables you to cope in a crisis?

Elizabeth: ... I think I've got resilience. I'm a very practical thinker. I can get things done. I can sort it.

Windy: Are you determined?

Elizabeth: Yes.

Windy: What would happen if you brought your resilience and your determination to developing the attitude, 'I don't like not knowing. I'd like to know. I don't need to know. Not knowing is uncomfortable but not terrible. It's not unbearable'? What would happen if you brought your resilience and your determination to developing those ideas?

Elizabeth: I think I'd be a less anxious person. I think I would enjoy life more. I wouldn't have this constant dread that I'm waiting for something. Well, it's not constant, it's a lot of the time that I'm waiting for something bad to happen to me. I think I would live in the moment more.

Windy: Yeah, that's right. And so, what I'm gonna suggest to you is daily practice of that idea and using every opportunity to face what you've been avoiding, because we know from your testimony that facing things has actually helped you to deal with this particular problem in the past. It's when you avoid, which is understandable because that's the empathetic bit. That's your first response. It doesn't have to be your last response, avoidance. What I say: avoid the avoidance. You can actually do a U-turn. But your first port of call's gonna be that, understandably, but it doesn't have to be the next port of call. And you can really say, 'Right, OK, let me face this. I don't like not knowing, but I can stand it and, if there is anything wrong, then I'll deal with it. And, if I do die, that would be tragic for me and the kids, but they will survive that.' And so, you can actually start to break the legacy that you were brought up with.

[*Here, I am covering a lot of ground: (i) Elizabeth's first response will be an anxious one based on her rigid and extreme attitude towards uncertainty; (ii) she can how herself empathy (one of her strengths) when this happens; (iii) face don't avoid; (iv) use determination and resilience to rehearse a flexible and non-extreme attitude towards uncertainty; (v) her daughters are resilient and will cope with her death and (vi) daily practice of this solution is needed. It would have been better if I had 'chunked' this into smaller separate response and get her opinion on each. Also, I needed to get a summary of thee points from Elizabeth to determine her understanding of these components her views about them.*]

Elizabeth: ... [*Pause*] Yeah, 'cos it a legacy, definitely.

Windy: Yeah, it sounds like a legacy.

Elizabeth: It is, yeah. And I know that I project a lot of my feelings towards my relationship with my mum towards them. I know I do that.

Windy: Yeah. What were some of your feelings about your mum that you're projecting, do you think? [**#SST 20**]

                 [*It is not unusual for a client to bring up other factors that emerge from the therapeutic discussion. It would have been better if I had asked Elizabeth if this was an important issue for us to discuss. I assumed it was.*]

Elizabeth: That I couldn't live without her, when something happened to her.

Windy: And what did you find out?

Elizabeth: It's been very difficult, like super-duper difficult, like horrendous, but it's five years on and I've got to live on for her. And she left me a letter anyway to make sure I did. So, I feel that I completely shocked myself. I feel quite emotional saying this now. But

... I've actually shocked myself that I ... do function without her.

Windy: Right. And how well do you function without her?

Elizabeth: I cry every day.

Windy: So did my mum.

Elizabeth: Yeah. I cry every day.... She's a very strong woman.

Windy: So, what can you take from that experience to actually function even better? What are some of the things that you may not be doing that you might consider doing for yourself? [**#SST 21**]

Elizabeth: ... [*Pause*] I suppose to face up to things, not avoid, and also ... [*pause*] it's like I want to change the narrative of what you've just said, of my adult children. I can start changing the narrative. My narrative, my story's mine with my mum and I don't want that legacy to carry on. I really don't.

Windy: No. But you did change your narrative. You've changed it. You're functioning. You shocked yourself. You're functioning. [**#SST 22**]

Elizabeth: Yes, I did.

Windy: And so, maybe you can shock yourself even more by doing things that would indicate, 'Hey, I'm functioning even more. And that's what I'm saying. Is there anything that you could be doing that would indicate that to you?

[*It seems important that Elizabeth can see that she has, as she says, projected her own difficulties coping without her mother onto her daughters. I introduce a new focus where she can cope even better without her mum.*]

Elizabeth: Yes. I think I would start to enjoy my life a bit more.

Windy: What kinds of things would you be doing?

Elizabeth: Going out more. I know what it is, it's doing the things... that I haven't done since she passed.

Windy: Like what?

Elizabeth: Looking at photos.

Windy: Of her?

Elizabeth: Yeah. Just enjoying her when she was well.

Windy: That's right, and also allowing yourself to be sad while you enjoy.

Elizabeth: Yeah.

Windy: It's both/and. It's not either/or.

Elizabeth: Yeah. It's going places that I avoid.

> [*Here, I help Elizabeth to see that developing the 'I can cope without my mother' narrative can be done by her facing up to experiences that she has previously avoided.*]

Windy: OK. Let's have a look at where you're avoiding that you would like to go.

Elizabeth: OK. A place?

Windy: Yeah.

Elizabeth: I'm from East London. My family are from East London.

Windy: Whereabouts?

Elizabeth: We're from Stepney.

Windy: OK. You're a Stepney girl?

Elizabeth: Yeah.

Windy: I'm a Hackney boy.

Elizabeth: Oh yeah, I know Hackney really well. So the
                  markets. My family were market traders and I want
                  to go back to those places where my mum went.

Windy: OK. So why don't you go? Do you have a mobile
                  phone? Here's my invitation: send me a picture of
                  you in Stepney.

Elizabeth: Yeah, I will do.

Windy: Send it to me by email. I'd love to see.

                  [*The role of 'place' in facilitating change in SST is
                  important (Dryden, 2024b). Elizabeth sent me the
                  photo that appears in Chapter 4.*]

Elizabeth: Yeah. I'd love to go back to our house.

Windy: Fine. And what do you think you'd feel by going
                  back to your house?

Elizabeth: I'd just feel more connected to my mum 'cos I'm
                  not burying it. I just wanna bring her back but in that
                  way.

Windy: Yeah, OK. And can you have that connection and
                  still recognise that she's dead?

Elizabeth: I don't use the word 'dead', but you've done it now.

Windy: Well, what do you use?

Elizabeth: Passed away.

Windy: Alright, that's fine.

Elizabeth: I do feel connected to her and I really do, yeah. I talk to her every day.

Windy: OK. Do you ever talk to yourself every day without talking to your mum?

Elizabeth: … She's always there, so I don't know. I think I do. Yeah, I do.

Windy: Moving forward, what kind of relationship do you want to have with your mum that's healthy for you and will aid you in dealing with your health anxiety?

   [*This is a key question since as the conversation deepen it increasingly seems that Elizabeth's current relationship with her late mother is an important factor here.*]

Elizabeth: I want to be a bit more adult to adult with her. I wanna be a bit more independent. She came to all hospital appointments. Obviously, I'm 58, so she died – I said it then – five years ago.

Windy: How does it feel to say it, by the way?

Elizabeth: … [*Long pause*] A bit weird to say it 'cos I don't say it.

Windy: Yeah. It just popped out.

Elizabeth: It just came out, yeah. I very rarely say it. I do sound very childlike when I say it 'cos even before she got ill she would come to the dentist with me, all doctors' appointments, everything.

Windy: And what do you think that said to you about your own resilience?

Elizabeth: I can't cope without her.

                [*Here, I help Elizabeth to see the relationship between her mother accompanying here at her health-related appointments and her own resilience.*]

Windy: Exactly. Now, do you go to your adult daughters' appointments with them?

Elizabeth: They don't let me, no.

Windy: They don't let you. But you would if you could?

Elizabeth: I would, but there's a part of me that I'm glad they do it 'cos I have brought them up that they do. So, I'm glad that they do do that.

Windy: So, I think that one of the things we've talked about, isn't it, this idea that you've developed that you thought at one point you couldn't do without your mum.

Elizabeth: Absolutely.

Windy: You're now learning that you can and that you want to have a more adult-to-adult relationship with her. What was her first name?

Elizabeth: Rita.

Windy: Can you call her Rita?

Elizabeth: Yeah, Rita.

Windy: In your conversations with her?

Elizabeth: Yeah, I could do. Rita.

Windy: Rather than what?

Elizabeth: Mum.

Windy: That's right. One way of having an adult relationship with your mum, to change the language. Call her Rita. What did she used to call you?

Elizabeth: My Angel.

Windy: Well, have her call you Elizabeth in this dialogue. You've got My Angel. And so, I think you have learnt, but even when you learnt it, you hadn't broken away. Now you can continue to actually have that more fun and have an adult relationship with your mum where you call her by her first name, not Mum and My Angel – Rita and Elizabeth. And then you can continue the legacy of showing your kids, your adult female children that they can get by without you and that you can get by without them. [**#SST 17b**]

[*I often suggest that people use their parents' first names in facilitating a change of relationship. Here I also suggest that in her conversations with her mum she thinks of her mother using her first name, rather than 'my angel'.*]

Elizabeth: Yeah.

Windy: And, if you did that and consistently do that, it will be very interesting to see what happens to your health anxiety, particularly if you also learnt to tolerate uncertainty, tolerate the wait and recognise that the way to deal with these things is as a book: Chapter 1 where you do have these initial reactions, but there's a Chapter 2, Chapter 3, Chapter 4 for you and a Chapter 1, Chapter 2, Chapter 3, Chapter 4 for them. [**#SST 16b**]

[In using my book analogy again, I show Elizabeth that there is a process for her and another one for her adult offspring.]

Elizabeth: Yeah.

Windy: OK. So, do you wanna summarise what we've done? [**#SST 23**]

[My sense is that we are reaching the end of our conversation. She has a solution and can rehearse it. However, it would have been better to highlight this more so that she could put it in her own words.]

Elizabeth: Yeah. For me to summarise?

Windy: Yeah. I'm too old to summarise.

[Use of humour again.]

Elizabeth: So, I started the session, presented to you that I've got dreadful health anxiety, couldn't live without my mum, worried about leaving my children if I'm ill and what are they gonna do and how are they gonna cope. My go-to emotion is to panic and think I'm gonna die or everything's gonna be catastrophic if something happens to me. But to get more into that adult part of me and to recognise my children are adults. To be less avoidant. To know that I can have that Chapter 2, and that's really resonated with me. To call my mum by her first name, to have that adult-to-adult relationship. I like what you said about avoid the avoidance. To be more... present and to try to accept the feelings I have with uncertainty. And that, basically, we will all cope because I have coped. I have coped without my mum being physically here. And I have coped and know that my children will cope if in the probability of whatever the probability is.

Windy: Of what?

Elizabeth: Of me becoming ill and them having to cope.

Windy: Yeah.

Elizabeth: I know they will cope.

Windy: You will die. We don't know where, we don't know when.

Elizabeth: We don't know when. Like that song that you said: *We don't know where, we don't know when.*

Windy: But, as you say, you're not scared of dying.

Elizabeth: No, not now.

Windy: No, because you brought your resilience and your determination, which are real strengths of yours, and you can take those with you to Stepney. You can take the determination and your resilience anywhere you wanna go.

Elizabeth: Yeah, and also the other part is for me to start to enjoy things. I do enjoy life, I do go out. It's not that I don't. It's just that I avoid places. But to enjoy my mum, the continuing bond I've got with her, if you like, to enjoy her before she was ill, where I haven't done that. To enjoy who she is and go to those places.

Windy: And, even though it might be painful, you can still go and rely on your resilience and your determination, because you will be taking those with you.

[In her summary, Elizabeth covers most of the points we discussed and what she will take away. I added one or two things to her summary which is not unusual, but the main points came from her. I did not ask Elizabeth for her takeaways because these were specified in her summary [#SST 24].

Elizabeth: Yeah, my resilience and also I can feel sad and happy as well in the same experience.

Windy: Absolutely, yeah. So, we didn't do much in our single session, did we? Thank you so much for having this conversation.

Elizabeth: Thank you so much.

[I did not ask Elizabeth my standard question at the end of the session (i.e. is there anything you want to ask me or tell me before we finish that you might regret not asking me or telling me once the session is over) because I had a sense that we had arrived at a good ending. Nevertheless, I regret not asking her that question [#SST 25].]

4

Elizabeth's Follow-Up Questionnaire

Follow-Up Questionnaire

Name: Elizabeth
Date: 02/06/2024

Please type your responses in the spaces provided.

Question Response

1. What progress did you make on the issue that you brought to the session. Indicate the amount of progress you have made on this issue by using a 0% (no progress) – 100% (problem solved) scale.	Issue Brought to the Session (Please name this): Health anxiety Amount of progress made: 55%

Factors that helped me make progress:

Windy assisting me with my issues in the present and how I can move forward with my issue, and not asking too many questions about where it started really helped as I know where it started and was happy not to tell my life story again in great detail. Staying in the present and gaining tools to deal with it in the moment and the future has been valuable and very helpful.

The session broadened into my relationship with my mum and my grief around her death, how I thought I wouldn't cope without her, couldn't live without her. He encouraged me to acknowledge my resilience and determination and the qualities I possess that have enabled me to cope and to recognise this. He suggested I sometimes call my mum by her name rather than 'mum', to enable an adult-to-adult connection. This helped as I always had separation anxiety with my mum, we were very close and enmeshed to a degree.

Being adult/adult with my mum gives me a feeling of control and confidence in myself, I feel like an adult.

Understanding more about the connection between avoidance and anxiety. Since the session I have had a blood test and another 2 health tests of which I usually avoid and am very scared to even book the appointment. Facing these tests and taking control of my health has empowered me to feel more responsible and less anxious.

First response and second response, Windy didn't dismiss my habitual first response, he understood it and encouraged me to have confidence in knowing I have the option of the second response and the second chapter can be different to the first chapter.

Talking about my children as 'adult women offspring' has helped me to associate them with their resilience and strength rather than vulnerable, needy children.

Having overcome my fear of death since my mum died, Windy said my determination and resilience has enabled this, and I can use these attributes to manage my health anxiety. I hadn't thought of it like that.

Talking more about the difference between worry and concern, remembering times I have been concerned and addressed health issues. Reminding me that I have faced things in the past and I have, at times, addressed some health issues without panic. That was a good reminder for me.

I find it very difficult to wait for test results, I am at times terrified. Windy explained that my attitude towards uncertainty has been the problem, more so that the actual uncertainty. Changing my language around uncertainty, using different words that are more realistic and rational, i.e. 'in all probability' rather than absolute certainty.

Acknowledging my own strengths and how they have helped with my life experiences has helped me to actually feel stronger.

Windy asked me to identify a goal for the near future, of which I did. It gave me something to aim for.

Breaking the legacy of how I was brought up in terms of health anxiety, worry and my attachment to my mum and continuing the legacy with my children of showing them a different narrative regarding this issue. Poignant and powerful for me! And how I have changed my narrative already from 'I'll never cope without my mum' to 'I'm functioning and enjoying life with the sadness there too'

Windy asked me to summarise the session instead of him of which helped me to reinforce what we had discussed in the session. In other

	counselling it's usually the therapist who sums up. I thought this was a good technique and helped me to embed some key points. **Factors that were absent that could have helped me make more progress:** None that come to mind.
2. Did you make any progress on other issues that you have that you did not bring to our session? Please elaborate.	I have also had anxiety when my adult daughters are out socialising and travelling home to their house on their own. I have their location on find friends on my iPhone. I was quite obsessive about looking at where they are on the location finder. It would cause anxiety and also sometimes bother my daughters too. I wouldn't go to sleep until I could see they were home, this could be 2 am at night. I have also called them on many occasions to check where they are and how they are getting home. Since my session with Windy and fully acknowledging that they are sensible, intelligent adults, and knowing this is

	also linked to uncertainty and my need to know they are safe and at home, I have significantly reduced the amount of time I track where they are. In the main, I go to sleep when they are out socialising. I seem to have more trust and acceptance; it feels quite freeing and liberating to gradually loosen the reigns of my needing to know and be in control.
3. How would you describe your relationship with Windy Dryden in the session?	To start with I felt apprehensive, his style of counselling is not something I am too familiar with. I soon felt very comfortable. I was able to switch off from the other attendees. It felt like a private individual session. There was a way that he didn't ask about my past too much, but when we did talk about it briefly and where my issues started, it felt very personal, familiar, safe and connected, as if he knew. I didn't feel the need to tell my whole story for Windy to understand me and my health anxiety.

4. What, if anything, did Windy Dryden do during the session that was helpful to you?	He asked me to summarise at the end of the session of which was very helpful, rather than him doing it. His humour helped and was appropriate. He asked me where my family hail from and this connected to some issues around my grief for my mum. I plan to visit this place and he asked me to send him a photo of when I visit. I have this planned for July 13th and I shall definitely send Windy a photo. I felt like he cared and was genuinely interested. Windy also mentioned his own mother and grandmother, which makes him human and therefore more relatable.
5. What, if anything, did Windy Dryden do during the session that was unhelpful to you?	N/A

6. How helpful did you find the pre-session form if you were sent one? Please elaborate.	N/A
7. How helpful did you find the audio-recording of your session? Please elaborate.	I was surprised at how much was covered in the one session. Listening to it enabled me to reflect more on what was said, more so than reading the transcript. I took notes when listening, which helped me to further digest the content of the session. Very helpful.
8. How helpful did you find the transcript of your sessions? Please elaborate.	It was useful to see our conversation in words. I was quite emotional reading it, it felt like I was having the session again. I hadn't remembered all of it. It has helped to reinforce what I learnt from the session with Windy.

9. How does Single-Session Therapy compare with other therapies that you have had? Please elaborate.	The single session covered a lot more than I thought it would. It was more solution focused than other therapy I have had. I like to build a relationship with a therapist and that usually takes time over several sessions. However just in that one session I did get the sense and feeling of a rapport with Windy. It was unrushed, and what surprised me most was how much was covered in that one session. Other therapy has been less solution focused and more psychodynamic, exploring my past, my attachment style and where it all began. How my past has informed my present. The single session with Windy was focused more towards giving me tools and techniques to deal specifically with my health anxiety and yet even though my past was not so much of the focus, with the little I said about it, he made it feel important and relevant.

10. What improvements, if any, do you think need to be made to the Single-Session Therapy framework?	The only feedback I have is that as this is a single session, if past traumas were unearthed in that session, and if it was a client's first experience of therapy, I would want to know that there is further support for them. I did research this and looked on Windy's website too and I can see that further support is usually offered.
11. Please give any additional feedback that your responses to the questions above have not covered.	During the session Windy asked me if I had a goal. I said I want to book my blood test and have it in March. I wasn't able to do it in March, I did avoid it. However, I had it on May 15th, so not too long after. I have had the results and all is ok. I feel more in control of my health now, more empowered and adult. Much less anxious because I faced it, of which we talked about in the session. I also mentioned that I find it hard to drive past the Doctor's surgery. I decided to start driving past and face it, but the road has been closed for road works since my session! So that's a goal for when the road opens again. However,

I did walk past it today and because I have faced having the blood test and some other tests, I felt far less anxious, which proves that avoidance certainly does cause anxiety.

5

Reflections and Concluding Remarks

In this final chapter, I will reflect on the session I had with Elizabeth (see Chapters 1 and 3) and her feedback on the session three months after we had it (see Chapter 4). I will then make some concluding remarks.

Reflections

In this section, I will reflect on a number of issues that come to mind after reviewing the session I had with Elizabeth and the reflections she made on her follow-up questionnaire and afterwards when I sent her the book manuscript to review.

The Working Alliance in SST with Clients Who Are Therapists

Many of the SST demonstrations that I have done have been with volunteers who are therapists. This is certainly the case with my work for Onlinevents and it was the case with Elizabeth. The main advantage of working with therapists as clients in SST is that they tend to be self-aware and have probably already considered some of the factors involved in the problem that they wish to discuss with me. They may even have discussed the issue in their own ongoing personal therapy, but the fact that they wish to discuss the issue with me indicates that they still have the problem, at least to some degree. The main disadvantages of working with therapists as clients are as follows. First, therapists may bring to the demonstration session ideas about what therapy should be like, which may well come into conflict with the practice of SST, at least the way that I practise it. Second, therapists may well be used to building a therapeutic relationship slowly with their own clients and building such a relationship slowly with their own therapists when they are clients.

The rapid approach to forming an alliance adopted by myself as an SST therapist may well be a culture shock for such therapists. Elizabeth mentioned this when she said on her follow-up form:

> '*To start with I felt apprehensive, his style of counselling is not something I am too familiar with.*'

Other therapist-volunteers have also mentioned this. Some, like Elizabeth, are able to adjust quickly:

> '*I soon felt very comfortable. I was able to switch off from the other attendees. It felt like a private individual session*'.

Others struggle because they prefer to go more slowly than is the case in SST, particularly when the same therapists are looking for a solution to their problems. This is not so much of a problem in non-demo SST, where further help is available when needed. However, it can be an issue in SST demonstrations, as discussed.

The same issue is true for some therapist-volunteers who struggle with the amount of questions that I tend to ask in the session.

My takeaway from this is to be more explicit at the outset about the way I tend to practise SST, particularly when a solution-focused approach is called for, as it very often is in such volunteer sessions. Thus, I might say something like:

> *'Before volunteering, bear in mind that we probably won't have time to develop our therapeutic relationship slowly. My goal is to help you focus on what you want to discuss with me and work with you to help you take away something meaningful from the session that will make a difference to you. To this end, bear in mind that I am likely to ask you quite a lot of questions.'*

Humour and Self-disclosure

Humour and self-disclosure are two features of my work in SST that, in my view, facilitate the development of a good work alliance between myself and my client. Elizabeth made reference to both factors in her follow-up questionnaire. Of my use of humour, she said on her follow-up questionnaire:

> *'His humour helped and was appropriate'*, and when discussing my use of self-disclosure, she said, *'Windy*

also mentioned his own mother and grandmother, which
made him human and therefore more relatable'.

How Much Ground to Cover in a Single Session

One of the dilemmas that single-session therapists experience is
how much ground to cover in a session. The pithy statements
'less is more' and 'more is less' encourage us to be conservative
concerning how much ground we cover with a client lest they be
overwhelmed with too much material. While this is good advice,
it should not be followed uniformly, for there are clients who are
able to process more in the session than others can. On this issue,
I am guided by a number of factors:

- The complexity of the issue the client has nominated.
  The more complex the issue, the more factors the client
  and I need to cover
- Whether I am rushing or not. If I find that I am rushing
  in the session, then I am pushing the client to cover too
  much material for them
- Whether, in my view, the client is processing what we
  are discussing. If I have the sense that the client is
  struggling to process what we are discussing, then we are
  covering too much material.

The client's summary shows what the client has retained from
the session and is a good guide concerning whether or not the
client and I have covered too much material.

If you recall, it is a feature of my SST demonstration work that after the session, I send the volunteer the audio recording of the session and later a typed transcript of it. These materials provide the volunteer with a reminder of what we discussed in the session. So, even if the person struggled to process everything in the session or forgot something, these materials can help them to remember and further process the issues that we discussed.

Referring to the recording, Elizabeth said on her follow-up form:

> *'I was surprised at how much was covered in the one session. Listening to it enabled me to reflect more on what was said, more so than reading the transcript. I took notes when listening of which helped me to further digest the content of the session. Very helpful.'*

Referring to the transcript, Elizabeth said, again on her follow-up form:

> *'It was useful to see our conversation in words. I was quite emotional reading it, it felt like I was having the session again. I hadn't remembered all of it. It has helped to reinforce what I learnt from the session with Windy.'*

The Ground that Elizabeth and I Covered in the Session

- The importance of staying in the present and gaining tools to deal with her problem in the moment.

- Recognising that she can cope without her mother and that her adult female offspring can cope without her.
- The importance of facing her fears and going for blood tests.
- Accepting her first problematic response and responding to it.
- Recognising that she can use her determination and resilience to deal with her health anxiety.
- Seeing the difference between worry and concern.
- Seeing that uncertainty is just not knowing and that the probability is that she is OK helps her to tolerate waiting for test results. Here, Elizabeth noted on reading the whole book that I sent her for comment:

'When I re-read the part about "in all probability", I again felt the same feeling I had when you were counselling me, I can only describe it as a settling feeling, I suppose acceptance too; so much more realistic and adult. And less the frightened child that I usually become with my health anxiety.'

As Elizabeth said, we covered a lot of ground in the session, more than she was expecting and if I am honest, more than I was expecting. The question remains whether we covered too much ground so that it adversely affected what Elizabeth took away from the session.

On this point, Elizabeth said as follows, having read the book manuscript that I sent her to review:

'When you talk about covering too much in the session, there was quite a lot covered, more than in other counselling sessions I've had. If I were to have another SST session with a therapist, I'd need to take notes either during it or directly afterwards, as I'd want to remember what was discussed. It wasn't too much for me during our session, but of course, I had the transcript sent to me to jog my memory. I am a note-taker anyway, so I would probably do this if I were to have another SST session.'

Progress and Generalisation

So, what effect did the session have on Elizabeth?

Progress

Using a subjective scale assessing how much progress she made on the issue we discussed, where 0% = no progress and 100% = problem solved, Elizabeth gave a rating of 55%. To me this indicates that she rated her problem as more than half solved. The session contributed to this rating, but in my view, it was what Elizabeth did subsequently that accounted most for her progress. Thus, she went for blood tests, which she had avoided, walked past her doctor's surgery, which she had also avoided doing and visited her childhood home in Stepney Green, which she had not done for many years. The purpose of the latter was to process her emotions and to develop a more adult-to-adult relationship with her late money. She promised to send me a photo of her at Stepney, and here it is.

In her accompanying email, Elizabeth said:

> *'We talked about me visiting where I lived with my mum when I was younger. I went there yesterday for the first time in many years, and here is the photo of me outside Stepney Green Station. It was quite emotional, but I'm glad I did it.'*

All this shows, I think, that with anxiety, what the person does after the single session will largely determine how much progress they will make. The role of the single session is to prepare the ground for subsequent action to address anxiety-related threats.

Generalisation

As I noted in Chapter 2, I did not broach the issue of how Elizabeth could generalise what she learned from the session to other areas because I thought that this might detract from what she would take away, given that we had covered a lot of ground in the session. In her follow-up questionnaire, Elizabeth proved me wrong. She mentioned that she had made progress in letting go of her anxiety concerning the whereabouts of her daughters when they are out. This showed that she applied the work we did on changing her relationship with her daughters with respect to health issues to this second issue, which we did not focus on in the session.

Concluding Remarks

The session that I have presented and analysed in the book is not a perfect illustration of Single-Session Therapy. I have shown in my commentary on the session in Chapter 3 the errors and omissions that I made in the session. However, it was a 'good enough' session of SST that gave Elizabeth an opportunity to discuss important factors that were central to her health anxiety issue and that were involved in her relationships with her late mother and her adult daughters. The latter issues were also relevant to her health anxiety.

The session also shows I believe the value of taking an individualised approach to health anxiety, in this case rather than a protocol-driven approach. The value of the former approach is that a single session with five clients seeking help with health anxiety will be different from one another, while in the latter approach, all five clients would be dealt with in a similar way. The former is in keeping with the spirit of SST, while the latter is not.

Finally, I hope I have shown how I merge interventions based on the single-session therapy mindset with those based on what I call my 'take' on the client's problem, informed as that is by concepts and techniques from REBT.

In closing, I do want to reiterate that this book is not designed to have you practise SST as I practise it. It is designed to help you see how you can integrate your own 'take' on anxiety with interventions that stem from the SST mindset. It is also designed to show what can be achieved in 39 minutes with a volunteer keen to get help with a distressing issue.

Appendix 1

Shared (underlined) and Distinguishing Components of Rigid/Extreme and Flexible/Non-extreme Attitudes

Components of a Rigid/Extreme Attitude	Components of a Flexible/Non-Extreme Attitude
Rigid Attitude *1. Preference* *2. Demand Asserted* 'I don't want my boss to criticise me and therefore he must not do so'	**Flexible Attitude** *1. Preference* *2. Demand negated* 'I don't want my boss to criticise me, but it does not have to be the way I want must not do so'
Awfulising Attitude *1. Evaluation of Badness* *2. Awfulising* 'It would be bad if my boss criticised me and therefore it would be the end of the world'	**Non-Awfulising Attitude** *1. Evaluation of Badness* *2.Non-Awfulising* 'It would be bad if my boss criticised me, but it would not be the end of the world'

Attitude of Unbearability	**Attitude of Bearability**
1. *Struggle* 2. *It's Unbearable*	1. *Struggle* 2. *It's Bearable* 3. *It's Worth It* 4. *I'm Worth It* 5. *Willingness to Bear It* 6. *Going to Bear It*
'It would be hard to bear if my boss criticised me, and therefore, I could not bear it'	'It would be hard to bear if my boss criticised me, but I could bear it, it is worth bearing, I am worth bearing it for, I am willing to bear it, and I am going to do so'
Devaluation Attitude	**Unconditional Acceptance Attitude**
1. *Negatively Evaluated Aspect* 2. *Asserted Devaluation (of self/other/life)*	1. *Negatively Evaluated Aspect* 2. *Negated Devaluation (of self/other/life)* 3. *Asserted Unconditional Acceptance (of self/other/life)*
'If my boss criticised me, that would be bad and would prove that I am an idiot'	'If my boss criticised me, that would be bad but would not prove that I am an idiot person. It would prove that I am a fallible human being capable of doing well and poorly'

Appendix 2

The Meaning of Rigid/Extreme Attitudes and Flexible/Non-Extreme Attitudes

Rigid and Extreme Attitudes	Flexible and Non-Extreme Attitudes
• **Inconsistent with reality, illogical, largely unconstructive**	• **Consistent with reality, logical, largely constructive**
Rigid	**Flexible**
• Demanding that my desire is met	• Preferring but not demanding that my desire is met
• Holding this attitude unconditionally	• Holding this attitude conditionally
• No exceptions are possible.	• Exceptions are possible
• Unable to adapt to changing circumstances	• Able to adapt to changing circumstances
• Unbending	• Able to bend
Awfulising	**Non-Awfulising**
• Recognising that it is bad if my desire is not met, and this means it is awful	• Recognising that it is bad if my desire is not met, but it is not awful
• Nothing could be worse	• Things could always be worse
• This adversity is more than 100% bad	• The adversity is less than 100% bad
• No good can possibly come from this adversity which is wholly bad	• Good can come from this adversity which is not wholly bad
• This adversity cannot be transcended	• The adversity can be transcended

Unbearable	Bearable
• Recognising that it is a struggle to bear the adversity and that I cannot bear it • I will die or disintegrate if the adversity continues to exist • I will lose the capacity to experience happiness if the adversity continues to exist	• Recognising that it is a struggle to bear the adversity but that I can bear it • While I will struggle if the adversity continues to exist, I will neither die or disintegrate • I will not lose the capacity to experience happiness if the adversity continues to exist. Although this capacity may be temporarily diminished • The adversity is worth bearing • I am worth bearing it for • I am willing to bear the adversity • I am going to bear the adversity • Acting on the above
Devaluation	**Unconditional Acceptance**
• It is possible to rate an aspect of a person or of life and this rating can also be applied to the whole of the person or to life • The worth of a person or of life depends on conditions that change	• It is possible to rate an aspect of a person or of life, but this rating cannot legitimately be applied to the whole of the person or to life. The reason is that (a) a person is unrateable, complex, fallible, unique and in flux and (b) life is unrateable, complex, in flux, unique in the moment and contains unrateable, complex, fallible, unique human beings who are in flux • The worth of a person or of life is fixed and does not depend on conditions that change

Appendix 3

Anxiety versus Non-Anxious Concern

Adversity	• You are facing a <u>threat</u> to your personal domain	
Basic Attitude	RIGID/EXTREME	FLEXIBLE/NON-EXTREME
Emotion	Anxiety	Concern
Behavioural Consequences	• You avoid the threat	• You face up to the threat without using any safety-seeking measures
	• You withdraw physically from the threat	• You stay in the situation and take constructive action to deal with the threat
	• You ward off the threat (e.g. by rituals or superstitious behaviour)	• You do not employ any attempts to ward off the threat. You see the value of facing it and dealing with it directly
	• You try to neutralise the threat (e.g. by being nice to people of whom you are afraid)	• You employ no neutralising methods preferring to deal with the threat directly if it happens

	• You distract yourself from the threat by engaging in other activity	• You face the threat if it occurs without distracting yourself from it
	• You keep checking on the current status of the threat hoping to find that it has disappeared or become benign	• You develop a plan to deal with the threat if it happens and get on with the business of living without checking on the status of the threat
	• You seek reassurance from others that the threat is benign	• You make your own mind up if the threat is benign. If it is, you go about your business. If it is not benign then you deal with it
	• You over-prepare in order to minimise the threat happening or so that you are prepared to meet it (NB it is the over-preparation that is the problem here)	• You prepare to meet the threat but do not over-prepare
	• You seek support from others to help you face up to the threat and rely on them to protect you from it by handling it for you	• You seek support from others to help you face up to the threat and then take constructive action by yourself rather than rely on them to handle it for you or to be there to rescue you

	• You tranquillise your feelings so that you don't think about the threat	• You think about the threat and remind yourself how you can deal with it and that you have the resources to do so. You do this without tranquillising your feelings
	• You overcompensate for feeling vulnerable by seeking out an even greater threat to prove to yourself that you can cope	• You deal with the threat as it is and accept your feelings of vulnerability as you do so. You do not overcompensate for feeling vulnerable by seeking a deal with a greater threat
Thinking Consequences	**Threat-exaggerated thinking**	
	• You overestimate the probability of the threat occurring	• You are realistic about the probability of the threat occurring
	• You create an even more negative threat in your mind	• You view the threat realistically
	• You ruminate about the threat	• You think about what to do concerning dealing with threat constructively rather than ruminate about the threat
	• You underestimate your ability to cope with the threat	• You realistically appraise your ability to cope with the threat

	• You magnify the negative consequences of the threat and minimise its positive consequences • You have more task-irrelevant thoughts than in concern	• You are balanced in your thinking about the negative and positive consequences of the threat • You have more task-relevant thoughts than in anxiety
	Safety-seeking thinking • You withdraw mentally from the threat • You try to persuade yourself that the threat is not imminent and that you are 'imagining' it • You think in ways designed to reassure yourself that the threat is benign or if not, that its consequences will be insignificant	

| | <ul><li>You distract yourself from the threat e.g. by focusing on mental scenes of safety and well-being</li><li>You over-prepare mentally in order to minimise the threat happening or so that you are prepared to meet it (NB once again it is the over-preparation that is the problem here)</li><li>You picture yourself dealing with the threat in a masterful way</li><li>You overcompensate for your feeling of vulnerability by picturing yourself dealing effectively with an even bigger threat.</li></ul> | |

References

Dryden, W. (2023). *Single-Session Therapy and Regret*. Onlinevents Publications.

Dryden, W. (2024a). *Single-Session Therapy and Procrastination*. Onlinevents Publications.

Dryden, W. (2024b). *Single-Session Therapy: 100 Key Points and Techniques. 2nd edition*. Routledge.

Dryden, W. (2025). Bringing a single-session mindset to counselling in an online health service in the UK. In Hoyt, M.F., & Cannistra, F. (eds). *Single Session Therapies: Why and How One-at-a-Time Mindsets Are Effective*. Routledge.

Makover, R.B. (2024). *Annotated Psychotherapy: A Session by Session Look at How a Therapist Thinks*. Routledge.

Ratner, H., George, E., & Iveson, C. (2012). *Solution Focused Brief Therapy: 100 Key Points and Techniques*. Routledge.

Index